Defying the Crescent

The Catholic King Who Saved Vienna

by

Dr. ant

Defying the Crescent: The Catholic King Who Saved Vienna

Contents

Introduction

In the annals of history, moments of profound significance often hinge upon the valor of a solitary figure or the unyielding faith of a devoted people. Such is the saga of John III Sobieski, the Catholic King, and the victories wrought in the name of Mary, where the strands of destiny and faith intertwine to shape the course of civilizations. The narrative unfolds against the backdrop of a Europe threatened by the swift expansion of the Ottoman Empire, a formidable force that seemed, at times, an inexorable tide poised to reshape the Western world.

The tale of Sobieski is not merely the chronicle of a warrior king but a testament to the indomitable spirit of Christendom in its darkest hours. As the Ottoman forces amassed, it was not only the skilled sword but also fervent prayer that steadied the hearts of those who would defend Vienna, a city of immense strategic allordance, indeed, but also a symbol of much greater consequence. The Siege of Vienna and its climactic battle reveal themes woven from the threads of faith, courage, and divine providence.

Reflecting on the broader canvas of history, this account demonstrates the pivotal role of individuals like Sobieski, who stand as bulwarks against the tides of adversity. His early life and reign reveal a man molded by divine allegiance and martial prowess, a combination that would render him not just a monarch but a legendary figure in the chronicles of both Poland and the Catholic faith.

The Siege of Vienna, a conflagration of military might and strategic ingenuity, serves as the crucible in which the mettle of Christian Europe was tested. The city's fortifications—both physical and spiritual—would withstand not only the bombardments of cannons but also the insidious siege of despair. It is here that Sobieski's strategic brilliance and his devotion to the Virgin Mary would illuminate the path to victory.

John Sobieski's march from Poland, replete with logistical hurdles and the relentless specter of urgency, further exemplifies the formidable resolve of this era's defenders. Every step of this harrowing journey forged an iron will necessary for the impending clash. The union of Sobieski's forces with those of the Holy League on the Feast of Our Lady's Assumption stands as a divine signpost, a convergence of sacred observance and martial determination.

As the battle commenced, it was a tapestry of tactical maneuvering and heroic stands, each skirmish and charge painting a vivid tableau of resistance against the encroaching Ottoman forces. Sobieski's leadership was not merely command but an embodiment of divine inspiration. His tactical decisions throughout the intensity of the conflict, balanced with his unwavering faith, heralded a triumph built not solely on human endeavor but on celestial support.

The resonant victory in Mary's Name resonates through subsequent history not just as a military success but as a symbol of an intrinsic belief in divine intervention. Key moments and turning points during the battle serve as testaments to the complex interplay between human agency and celestial favor. Even in the harrowing aftermath, the triumph was viewed through the prism of Providence, intertwining earthly events with heavenly ordination.

Yet, the turning of tides at the Siege of Vienna rippled far beyond the immediate joy of reprieve. The Ottoman Empire, once perceived as an unstoppable juggernaut, found itself retreating into a series of defeats that would culminate in the Treaties of Carlowitz and Passarowitz, reshaping not merely borders but the sociopolitical landscapes of entire civilizations.

Thus, the legacy of John III Sobieski is etched not just in the annals of Poland or the battlefields of Vienna but in the broader narrative of Western civilization and Christendom. His contributions transcend mere conquests, embodying a resurgence of Christian faith and a reaffirmation of divine justice. Sobieski's devotion to Mary reflects a potent fusion of martial and spiritual commitment, a beacon to the faithful and a bulwark against heretical forces.

John Sobieski's life and victories underscore profound themes of conviction and resilience that ripple through the historical and spiritual terrains of our shared humanity. His story reminds future generations of the inherent power of faith when united with valor. As Christendom faced perhaps one of its greatest threats from the Ottoman Empire, it emerged not only with its territories intact but its spiritual core emboldened. The victories in Mary's name signify not just temporal triumphs but eternal reminders of the strength drawn from divine intercession.

The triumph of faith over adversity and the long-term effects of these events on Europe cannot be overstated. The battle marked more than a military victory; it was a clarion call to Christian Europe, a reaffirmation of communal identity and shared purpose. The significance of Marian devotion reveals a spiritual facet deeply ingrained in the historical consciousness of the era, guiding the moral compass and fortifying the resolve of Christendom.

This introductory passage sets the stage for a more granular exploration within subsequent chapters, each delving into the nuanced preludes, conflicts, and resolutions that characterize this epochal moment in history. In these pages, the interwoven lives of saints and warriors, kings and commoners, converge into a narrative that is at once historical and philosophical, particular and universal.

As history unfolds, each chapter is an invocation to understand how the seeds of faith and valor sown by figures like John Sobieski and the legions dedicated to Mary's cause, germinated into the resilient bastions of civilization and Christendom. The effects of their sacrifices and victories continue to resonate, guiding not just historical scholarship but also informing the moral landscape of contemporary society.

Let us journey then, through the shadows of conflict and the illumination of divine favor, to grasp not only the historical verities but the timeless truths reflected in the mirror of the past. Herein lies the ultimate significance of the victories in Mary's Name and Jon Sobieski's indelible contribution to the grand tapestry of our shared human story.

Chapter 1: Prelude to Conflict

As the 16th century dawned, the ominous shadows of the Ottoman Empire's expansion cast a foreboding gloom upon a fractious Europe. Sultan after sultan unfurled a relentless campaign of conquest, stretching their imperial ambitions across continents. The Christian kingdoms, beleaguered and oft-splintered by internal discord, perceived the encroaching threat with a mix of dread and determination. The Mediterranean, once a cradle of Western civilization, became a troubled frontier where naval skirmishes and land battles were preludes to grander conflicts. Europe, a tapestry of faith and fealty, knit itself tighter under the aegis of the Church, awaiting the inevitable clash that would pit the Cross against the Crescent. Thus, Catholics and kings alike girded themselves, their prayers mingling with preparations, setting the stage for a conflagration that would resonate through the annals of history.

The Ottoman Empire's Expansion

In the annals of history, the Ottoman Empire's ascension from a mere Anatolian beylik to a sprawling dominion that straddled three continents is a tale that evokes both awe and trepidation. The ferocity and disciplined ambition with which they expanded their territories laid a foundation for centuries of imperial hegemony. This surge, deeply rooted in their military prowess and administrative acumen, would ultimately set the stage for myriad conflicts with an ever-vigilant Christendom.

Born in the late 13th century under the leadership of Osman I, the Ottomans initially captured the surrounding Byzantine territories, exploiting the waning power of the once-mighty empire. Their methodical and relentless expansionism proved successful, culminating in the dramatic fall of Constantinople in 1453 under Mehmed II. This conquest sealed the fate of the Byzantine Empire, transforming Istanbul—formerly Constantinople—into the heart of Ottoman power, and signaling a seismic shift in the balance between East and West.

The fall of Constantinople was more than a military triumph; it was a symbolic victory that screamed the Ottomans' intent to dominate. By controlling this storied city, the Ottoman sultans not merely amassed wealth and strategic advantage but revealed their ideological aspirations to lead the Islamic world. Their subsequent patronage of religious edifices and cultural institutions only reinforced their claim to be the new torchbearers of Islamic civilization. While Europe convulsed in shock and horror, the Ottomans set their sights deeper into the heart of Christendom.

As the Ottoman army grew in both might and sophistication, they employed a balanced blend of cavalry, infantry, and artillery—the likes of which had rarely been seen. The janissaries, an elite infantry corps composed of Christian youths converted to Islam, were integral to the empire's expansion. These soldiers, bound by fierce loyalty and rigorous military training, were the spearhead in many battles that brought terror upon European lands. The Ottomans' ingenuity in logistics, statecraft, and siege warfare made them a formidable adversary.

Throughout the 16th and 17th centuries, the Ottomans consistently locked horns with European forces across varied fronts. Their relentless campaigns led to the capture of key Balkan territories, Hungary, and parts of Eastern Europe. One cannot overstate the psychological impact of these incursions on Europe. To the devout Roman Catholic, the Ottoman threat was not simply a territorial contest; it was a cosmic struggle between the forces of Islam and Christendom. Clerics described the Ottomans as the scourge sent by divine providence to test the faithful.

At the heart of this expansion was the belief in 'ghaza'—the holy war. Though initially a unifying banner for the nascent empire, it later morphed into a complex interplay of political ambition and religious zeal. The sultans wielded it as both a divine mandate and a practical tool to stir the collective conscience of the populace. This dual motive made the Ottomans uniquely resilient and adaptable, enabling their incessant conquests even in the face of formidable coalitions.

The Mediterranean, too, felt the brunt of Ottoman expansionism. The siege of Rhodes in 1522 and the Battle of Lepanto in 1571 stand as vivid reminders of the ferocity and reach of Ottoman naval might. Though the Ottomans faced a resounding defeat at Lepanto, their maritime ambitions persisted, leaving an indelible mark on the trade routes and political landscape of the Mediterranean basin. These maritime ventures not only secured economic advantages but also served as a persistent reminder of the Ottoman grip around European throats.

One cannot discuss Ottoman expansion without acknowledging their innovative administrative structures. The millet system, which granted a degree of autonomy to various religious communities, showcased the Ottomans' pragmatic governance. Such a system not only ensured the loyalty of diverse populations but also stymied potential revolts. By allowing Christians and Jews to manage their internal affairs while paying jizya (a tax levied on non-Muslims), the Ottomans fostered a relative peace in their multi-ethnic empire, much to the consternation of European powers struggling with religious uniformity.

However, this relentless expansion was not without its perils. The sheer scale of the empire rendered it vulnerable to administrative inefficiencies and logistical nightmares. The further the Ottomans advanced into Europe, the more stretched their resources became. Additionally, internal dissent and succession crises frequently stymied their progress. Yet, these hindrances did not deter the Ottomans from eyeing Vienna—the golden apple of Europe.

Vienna's strategic significance cannot be understated. Positioned at the crossroads of trade routes, it represented both a prize and a gateway to the heart of Europe. Suleiman the Magnificent's failed siege in 1529 proved that Vienna was not an easy target. However, the sting of that failure lingered in the Ottoman psyche, culminating in another, more concerted effort in 1683. This time, they were better prepared, and Europe quivered under the looming shadow of their approach.

Europe's response, impelled by dread and desperation, would eventually lead to one of the most dramatic moments in the annals of Christian and Ottoman history. The Siege of Vienna in 1683 combined religious fervor, political strategy, and individual heroism, crystallizing an age-old conflict between cross and crescent. The significance of the imminent conflict broadened beyond mere territorial gain; it called into question the very survival of Christian Europe.

Thus, the scene was set for an epic clash, a prelude fraught with historical significance and divine invocation. John III Sobieski's eventual intervention would not only become a beacon of hope for Christendom but would also delineate the limits of Ottoman expansion. The events that transpired would be enshrined as a turning point, reverberating through the annals of European history for centuries to come.

Continuing to press forward despite numerous obstacles, the Ottoman Empire embodied a paradox—undaunted conquerors shadowed by vulnerabilities. The stage for conflict was larger than battlegrounds; it was splayed across the religious, cultural, and ideological canvas of the time. This empire's vast sweep from Anatolia to the gates of Vienna demanded a response, a unified counter that would reverentially be tied to faith, sovereignty, and the enduring spirit of Christendom.

Europe's Response to the Ottoman Threat

As the shadow of the crescent moon stretched across the landscape of Europe, the Christian nations found themselves confronting a formidable foe in the Ottoman Empire. The reach of Suleiman the Magnificent had unsettled the serene balance, and the specter of Ottoman domination loomed large. Europe, a mosaic of kingdoms and principalities, had to grapple with the necessity of a cohesive response to this existential threat. The intrigues of courts and councils played out amidst sacred edifices and hallowed halls, where orations and strategies were formulated with an urgency hitherto unseen.

One of the earliest signs of Europe's awakening to the Ottoman menace was in the diplomatic overtures and alliances that sought to unite a fragmented Christendom. The Holy Roman Empire, under the stewardship of Emperor Charles V, became a focal point of resistance. With the weight of both secular and sacred authority, Charles galvanized various German principalities, the Kingdom of Spain, and the Papal States. This assembly, albeit fraught with internal disputes, recognized the Ottoman threat as a common enemy that could no longer be ignored.

In the hustle and bustle of this formal congregation, one could hear the steady footsteps of messengers and the fervent prayers of clerics. The Councils convened, driven by a renewed sense of Christian solidarity. Decrees and edicts were issued, calling for fasting and penance, beseeching divine intervention against the imminent invasion. Such piety underpinned the broader strategic efforts, illustrating how faith and fortitude were interwoven in Europe's response.

Across this tumultuous scene, the Papacy emerged as a beacon of spiritual leadership and material support. Pope Pius V, with an iron resolve rooted in divine providence, was pivotal in rallying the Holy League—a coalition of Christian states determined to repulse the Ottoman advance. The Holy See's coffers were opened, and financial aid flowed to fortify the defenses of embattled cities and towns. The Pope's missives, laden with embodied conviction, called the faithful to arms.

Among the varied voices raised in this chorus of resistance, one must not overlook the smaller, but no less resolute, principalities and kingdoms. Venice, with its maritime prowess, recognized the Ottoman threat not merely as a danger to its sovereignty but also to Christendom's very essence. Venetian galleys, sleek and swift, patrolled the Mediterranean waters, intercepting Ottoman incursions and securing vital trade routes. The Venetian Doge's court, wreathed in the scent of salt and sea, echoed with preparations for war.

Yet, Europe's response was not solely martial. The intellectual and cultural bastions of the continent also girded themselves. Scholars and theologians, seated in cloisters and academies, penned treatises illuminating the ideological dichotomy between Christendom and the Ottoman worldview. These texts, disseminated widely, reinforced the narrative of a looming crusade—a defense not just of territory, but of the very principles of Christian civilization.

Among the celebrated figures who embodied this spirit of defiance was King John III Sobieski of Poland. His veneration of the Virgin Mary and unwavering commitment to the Christian cause elevated him to the status of a chivalric icon. Sobieski's correspondence with other European rulers underscored his steadfast faith and readiness to lead a united front against the Ottomans. His missives conveyed both a martial ardor and a spiritual zeal, elements that would later coalesce in his heroic defense of Vienna.

In the annals of European history, the response to the Ottoman threat stands as a testament to the improbable union of diverse, often discordant entities. The sceptered hands of monarchs, the mitred heads of bishops, and the scholarly frames of academics all contributed to a multifaceted bulwark. Whether through the clash of swords or the eloquence of sermons, Europe marshaled its myriad strengths into a resistance that was both corporeal and celestial.

It was within this cauldron of conflict and cooperation that the strategies were devised which would later unfurl upon the plains of Vienna. The Holy League convened, not merely as an amalgamation of armed forces but also as a sacred fraternity imbued with a sense of manifest destiny. The pages of history turned with the weight of their resolve, inscribed with ink that declared an unyielding commitment to repel the Ottoman advance and safeguard the sanctity of Christendom.

Thus, Europe's response to the Ottoman threat was more than an alignment of armies; it was a profound, collective affirmation of identity and purpose. With battlements as its bulwarks and prayers as its bulwarks, Christendom confronted the Ottoman menace with a unity forged in the foundries of faith and valor. This indomitable spirit would echo through the centuries, resonating in the annals of history and the collective memory of a continent bound together in its darkest hour.

Chapter 2: The Manichaean Challenge

The clash against Manichaeism presented an arduous trial for the Roman Catholic Church, summoning forth a spiritual and doctrinal battleground. Manichaeism, a syncretic religion blending elements of Christianity, Zoroastrianism, and Gnosticism, threatened to erode the doctrinal purity and unity of Christendom. The Church Fathers, with determined resolve, embarked on a multifaceted campaign to root out this heresy, utilizing theological discourses, council decrees, and pastoral initiatives. In such an era of spiritual turbulence, the need for a fortified and resilient Christendom became ever more pressing, lest the very foundation of Roman Catholicism buckle under the strain of dualistic heresies. The overarching struggle against Manichaean doctrines not only fortified the Church's theological pillars but also prepared it for the forthcoming trials posed by external foes, thus setting the grounds for triumphant victories in Mary's Name and the valorous interventions of John III Sobieski. The integral challenge lay in reaffirming the orthodoxy that would steer the faithful through the tempestuous seas of doctrinal deception and into the safe harbor of unwavering Catholic truth.

Origins of Manichaeism

The light and shadow of Manichaeism, that ancient and contentious doctrine, arose in the third century AD like a sepulchral chant echoing across the deserts of Mesopotamia. Founded by the Persian prophet Mani, the religion sought to weave a tapestry that combined the threads of Zoroastrian, Christian, and Buddhist beliefs. From the outset, Manichaeism was both a philosophical challenge and a theological thorn to the early Christian Church. In the context of our narrative, this mysterious faith represents a backdrop against which the steadfast devotion to orthodox Christianity was tested and ultimately fortified.

Mani, whose life and writings were as enigmatic as the faith he propagated, hailed from a noble Parthian family. His inspirations were manifold, drawing from the sacred texts of Zoroastrianism, the canonical works of Christianity, as well as Buddhist teachings. The dualism central to Manichaeism posited an eternal struggle between Light and Darkness, Good and Evil. This dichotomy, while appealing in its simplicity, threatened to undermine the Church's teachings on the unity and omnipotence of God. In Mani's vision, human existence itself was a battleground, a ceaseless contest between the ethereal forces of light and the malign, earthly shadows of darkness.

This burgeoning faith spread with alarming rapidity. From the sands of Persia, it reached the teeming marketplaces of the Roman Empire, the avenues of Carthage, and even the distant shores of China. Its allure lay in its comprehensive cosmology and stringent ethical code. Unlike many contemporaneous religions, Manichaeism offered a clear and compelling narrative of cosmic conflict, one that resonated with the human proclivity for moral dualism. However, such teachings were anathema to the orthodoxy of the early Church Fathers. They saw in Mani's doctrines a virulent heresy that threatened to dilute the purity of Christian doctrine and destabilize the moral and spiritual fabric of Christendom.

The theological battlegrounds were as intense as any physical confrontation could be. The Church, recognizing the danger posed by

Manichaean doctrine, mobilized its intellectual and spiritual resources to combat this heretical foe. The writings of Augustine of Hippo, himself a former adherent of Manichaeism, serve as both a repudiation and a testament to the influence of this dualistic creed. Augustine's eventual conversion to Christianity and his subsequent denunciation of Manichaeism signify a turning point in the struggle against this insidious heresy.

In its essence, Manichaeism also challenged the ecclesiastical structures of the time. It proposed a new and independent ecclesia, a community of the Elect and the Hearers, which stood in direct opposition to the clerical hierarchy of the Church. This ecclesiastical insurgency was perceived as a direct threat to the unity and authority of the Christian community, necessitating a robust and unwavering response from ecclesiastical authorities. Councils and synods convened to denounce Mani's teachings, and efforts to re-convert Manichaeans were redoubled.

The tale of Saint Augustine serves as a particularly poignant chapter in this struggle. Born in 354 AD in Roman North Africa, Augustine embraced the Manichaean faith during his youth, captivated by its promise of philosophical enlightenment and spiritual salvation. However, his intellectual journey led him ultimately to find solace and truth in Christianity. His conversion, profoundly documented in his writings, symbolizes a powerful triumph of orthodox thought over heretical subversion. Augustine's subsequent work, particularly "Confessions" and "City of God," holds a mirror up to the inherent contradictions and spiritual deficiencies of Manichaeism, fortifying the theological ramparts against this dualistic encroachment.

Manichaeism's spread to the farthest corners of the known world also compounded the Church's challenge. In the east, it found fertile ground among the settled communities of Central Asia and China, where it mingled with local religious traditions. Thus, the struggle was not merely confined to the Roman Empire but extended to regions less accessible to the Church's influence. The challenge then was twofold: to combat the heresy within the heartlands of Christianity and to stymie its growth in distant territories.

Moreover, the austere ethical demands imposed by Manichaeism added a layer of complexity to its appeal. Ascetic practices such as strict fasting, celibacy, and the denunciation of material possessions resonated with those seeking a purer, more devout spiritual path. These practices mirrored in some ways the ascetic traditions within Christianity, yet their underlying dualistic rationale deviated significantly from Christian theology. This convergence and divergence created a paradoxical landscape where truth and heresy often walked in uneasy proximity, necessitating discernment and unwavering faith from the defenders of orthodoxy.

As centuries passed, the influence of Manichaeism waned, but not without leaving an indelible imprint on the religious and cultural substrate of many regions. Its decline was hastened by relentless persecution and the theological counteroffensives mounted by the Church. Edicts and decrees, issued by both ecclesiastical and secular authorities, sought to extirpate the remnants of this once-flourishing faith. Despite this, the echoes of Manichaean thought can be discerned in later medieval heresies, such as the Cathar movement, which too propagated a dualistic view of the cosmos.

In this unfolding drama, Manichaeism serves as a stark portent of the challenges faced by Christendom in maintaining doctrinal purity and ecclesial unity. The vigorous efforts to counteract its spread—through theological discourse, ecclesiastical rulings, and even coercive measures —reflect the Church's determination to uphold the integrity of the faith. The history of this heresy underscores the perpetual vigilance required to shield the light of orthodoxy from the encroaching shadows of dualistic heresy.

Thus, the origins of Manichaeism and the Church's combative stance against it represent a critical nexus in the broader narrative of Christendom's trials and triumphs. Through understanding this ancient heresy and the enduring efforts to quash it, one gains a deeper appreciation for the historical resilience and theological depth of Christian orthodoxy. This narrative thread, weaving through the tapestry of history, contributes significantly to our understanding of the broader struggle to defend and propagate the Catholic faith, a struggle epitomized by the victories achieved in the unwavering name of Mary and the indomitable spirit of John Sobieski.

Catholic Efforts to Combat Heresy

The specter of heresy loomed large over Christendom during the rise of Manichaeism, a dualistic belief system that posited a cosmic struggle between light and darkness. This pernicious doctrine, which claimed adherents across the Roman Empire and beyond, was perceived as a dire threat to the unity and orthodoxy of the Catholic Church. The ecclesiastical authorities, ever vigilant in their custodianship of the true faith, marshaled considerable resources and embarked on multifaceted campaigns to root out and suppress this heretical movement.

Understanding the gravity of the Manichaean challenge requires us to delve into the larger context of the Church's struggle against heresy. This wasn't merely a religious skirmish but an existential battle for the soul of Christianity. Manichaeism presented a theological and philosophical conundrum that challenged the very core of Catholic doctrine, suggesting dualities that contradicted the monotheistic principles of the faith.

In response, the Catholic Church employed a combination of intellectual rigor and ecclesiastical authority. Prominent theologians like St. Augustine, himself a former adherent of Manichaeism, became pivotal figures in articulating a robust refutation of its tenets. Through his works, "Confessions" and "City of God," Augustine provided not only a personal testament to his conversion but also a compelling critique of Manichaean beliefs, highlighting their inconsistencies and moral failings.

The Church's efforts were not limited to theological debates. Ecclesiastical councils played a crucial role in formalizing the condemnation of Manichaeism. The Council of Arles in 353 AD and subsequent synods categorically denounced the heresy, issuing edicts that called for the excommunication of its adherents and the confiscation of their property. These decrees were enforced with varying degrees of severity across the empire, depending on the local rulers' disposition and the strength of the Manichaean presence.

The legal machinery of the Roman state was also co-opted in this holy war against heresy. Emperors like Diocletian and Constantine issued laws that criminalized the practice of Manichaeism, rendering it a punishable offense. Such statutes were designed to dismantle the organizational structures of the Manichaean communities, making it increasingly difficult for them to propagate their teachings and sustain their practices.

Yet, force alone was insufficient to obliterate this heresy. The Church recognized the need for pastoral care and conversion. Clerics were tasked with the arduous mission of re-educating former Manichaeans, guiding them back to the fold through catechesis and sacramental life. This pastoral approach was aimed at healing wounds and fostering a reintegration rather than merely punishing the wayward.

It is worth noting that the fight against Manichaeism was but a precursor to later, more extensive campaigns against other heresies. The methodologies established during this period—public disputation, ecclesiastical decrees, and state involvement—laid the foundation for future inquisitorial practices. The Inquisition, in its various forms, would draw upon the precedents set during the Manichaean crisis to combat subsequent departures from orthodoxy with even greater zeal.

Additionally, the Catholic Church harnessed the power of hagiography to champion the saints who stood firm against heresy. Stories of martyrs and confessors who resisted Manichaean pressures served both as moral exemplars and as tools of catechesis. These narratives reinforced the Church's teachings and inspired the faithful to remain steadfast in the face of doctrinal deviations.

No lesser significance should be attributed to the role of monasticism in this battle. Monasteries became bastions of orthodoxy, where the rigors of ascetic life and the discipline of communal living provided a stark contrast to the perceived excesses and errors of heretical groups. Monks devoted themselves to copying and preserving orthodox texts, ensuring that the true teachings of the Church were available for future generations.

Indeed, the convergence of theological acumen, pastoral sensitivity, legal enforcement, and monastic commitment forged a formidable arsenal against the heresy of Manichaeism. As we reflect upon these efforts, it becomes evident that the Church's response was as much about safeguarding the doctrinal purity as it was about preserving the unity of the Christian community in an era fraught with spiritual turmoil and diverse belief systems.

The eventual decline of Manichaeism in the West can be credited, in large part, to these Catholic efforts. By the time of the early medieval period, the visibility and influence of Manichaean communities had waned significantly, relegated to the annals of ecclesiastical history. However, the legacy of this struggle endured, shaping the Church's subsequent engagements with heretical movements and informing its broader mission of evangelization and doctrinal preservation.

In the grand tapestry of Catholic history, the ordeal of combating Manichaeism stands as a testament to the Church's resilience and adaptability. It highlights the enduring commitment to uphold the truths of the Christian faith and to counteract forces that seek to distort or undermine it. In a world ever susceptible to doctrinal confusion and moral ambiguity, the lessons gleaned from this epoch remain profoundly relevant.

Thus, as we continue our exploration of the Church's historical confrontations and triumphs, we must appreciate the multifaceted strategies that underpinned these efforts. The campaign against Manichaeism was not merely a defensive maneuver but an affirmation of the Church's divine mandate to teach, sanctify, and govern in accordance with the eternal truths entrusted to it by Christ.

Chapter 3: Dominic Guzman's Early Life and Mission

Emerging from the humble hamlet of Caleruega, Spain, Dominic Guzman, who would later be anointed Saint Dominic, was graced with intellect and piety from an early age. His mother, the venerable Juana of Aza, envisioned his future sanctity through divine dreams, foretelling a luminous path of service to Christendom. Ever ardent in his quest for divine truth, Dominic pursued theological studies at the esteemed University of Palencia, where his profound faith began to intertwine with scholarly rigor. Witnessing the pernicious spread of heresies, such as that of the Albigensians, Dominic's heart yearned for a reformation rooted in veritas and caritas. Thus, he founded the Order of Preachers, or Dominicans, purposing their mission to illuminate orthodoxy through preaching, teaching, and exemplifying Christ's love. His nascent order would, in due course, become a vanguard in the Church's defense against burgeoning heterodoxies, embedding his legacy indelibly in the annals of ecclesiastical history.

The Birth of a Saint

The seraphic light of a nascent dawn cast its gentle rays over the small town of Caleruega, nestled in the heart of Castile. The town, humble and unassuming, found itself marked by divine providence on the eve of Dominic Guzman's birth. Born in 1170 to noble and pious parents, Felix Guzman and Jane of Aza, Dominic's arrival was seen as a celestial beacon foretelling a life destined for holiness. His parents, well aware of the exigencies of nobility, did not merely foster an environment of privilege but instilled in their progeny the virtues of charity and unwavering faith.

In the stillness of the night, it's said that his mother, Jane, had a dream. In this vision, she beheld an awe-inspiring sight—a dog leaping from her womb, blazing with a torch in its mouth meant to set the world afire. An uncanny symbol, the dream heralded a mission that Dominic would later embody: to illuminate the contours of Christendom with the light of truth and quench the flames of heresy. The prophetic nature of Jane's vision was not lost upon those who discerned Dominic's path; it would become a bedrock of the Dominican emblem, a divine testimony of his sanctified mission.

Dominic's life unfolded in a tapestry woven with threads of austerity and scholarship. From an early age, he displayed a precocious intellect and a theological curiosity that endeared him to religious scholars and simple townsfolk alike. His initiation into the ecclesiastical world was swift. At the age of seven, he was entrusted to the care of his maternal uncle, a priest, who began his formal education in a school of letters and divine wisdom. The boy's prodigious talents soon flourished within the sacred precincts of the cathedral school of Palencia, where he absorbed the scriptures, philosophy, and the adamantine codes of church dogma.

The years spent in Palencia were transformative. His comrades and professors alike noticed his singular commitment to the scriptures, his assiduous pursuit of knowledge coupled with a heart brimming with compassion. A relentless scholar, he preferred the illumination of holy texts to worldly distractions, spending countless nights in vigil and prayer, meditating upon the divine mysteries. It was here, amid the scholastic rigor and the spiritual fervor, that Dominic's resolute spirit was forged.

His ascendance was marked not by grandeur but by humility and service. A calling swept through Palencia that sent ripples of urgency; a famine afflicted the land, aggrieving the populace. Dominic, moved by profound empathy, purportedly sold his precious and erudite scrolls to feed the hungry, quipping, "I must study from those shelves which can teach how to feed the starving souls." This act of benevolence would be a harbinger of his lifelong dedication to the corporeal and spiritual welfare of humanity.

In his early twenties, he was ordained a canon regular of the Cathedral of Osma, a vocation that ushered him into a life sanctified by rule and prayer. The canons regular saw in Dominic not merely a devoted cleric but a luminary destined to lead. His virtues of charity, chastity, and obedience were not mere observances but a divine ethos emanating from his very being. Under the aegis of Bishop Diego de Acebo, the cathedral's ecclesiastical missions took on a new vigor with Dominic as a quintessential exemplar of piety and dedication.

Yet, it was upon the broader canvas of Christendom's spiritual exigencies that Dominic would etch his indelible mark. The epoch was marred with the ascendant Manichaean challenge, notably manifest in the Albigensian heresy. A fortuitous mission to Denmark with Bishop Diego to arrange a royal marriage catalyzed a deeper purpose. Along their journey, they encountered the stark reality of the Albigensian heresy ravaging the coteaux of southern France. It was a theological dualism that starkly opposed the corpus of Catholic orthodoxy, propagating views that disparaged the material world and enkindled divisive doctrines.

Confronted with heretical defiance and the imminent danger it posed to the unity of the Church, Dominic resolved to combat it not with the sword but with the word. Bishop Diego shared this ecclesiastical ardor, and they embarked on a seminal endeavor in the Languedoc region. The duo adopted a mendicant lifestyle, repudiating worldly possessions to exemplify the purity and asceticism of early apostolic times. They engaged in disputations, preaching with fervor, and embodying the very tenets of the faith they sought to defend.

It was here, amid the turbulent waters of theological dissent, that "The Birth of a Saint" truly commenced. Dominic's strategy was marked by a profound simplicity and luminous wisdom—he lived among the people, debated with the heretics, offered compassion to the confused, and ceaselessly prayed for divine intercession. His mission was not ephemeral but laid the groundwork for what would become the Order of Preachers, the Dominicans.

Thus, the foundational principles of his future Order were crystalline in this prenatal phase—the zeal for veritas (truth), the emphasis on scholastic excellence, and a lifestyle of apostolic poverty. Dominic's visionary approach set a precedent in the annals of church history. He sought to equip his friars not merely with rhetoric but with an incorruptible love for the truth, to traverse lands far and wide, igniting souls with the light of divine wisdom and quelling the shadows of ignorance.

The intricacies of Dominic Guzman's nascent life offer an effulgent prelude to a mission that would reconfigure the spiritual topography of an era. His birth was not merely an event but an epoch recalibrated by divine ordinance. From the serene pastures of Caleruega to the ecclesiastical rigor of Palencia and the turbulent debates in Languedoc, Dominic's formative years encapsulate the germination of a saintly mission aligned with celestial intents.

Dominic's path was marked by the indelible imprimatur of divine will, a testament to the sanctity that was to illuminate Christendom. As we navigate the resplendent corridors of his early life, the symbolism of his mother's dream becomes ever more poignant—a torchbearer destined to cast the flame of truth across shadowed lands. Thus, in Dominic Guzman, the Church found not merely a luminary but a guardian of truth, a sentinel against heretical aberration, and a paragon of apostolic virtue.

Founding the Dominicans

In the twelfth century, as the sun-dappled lands of Castile bore witness to the quiet birth of a visionary named Dominic Guzman, few anticipated the seismic shift his life's mission would herald for Christendom. Born to a noble family in Caleruega, Dominic's early years were steeped in the rich tapestry of Catholic devotion, scholarly pursuit, and an ardent zeal for truth. Such a foundation prepared him well for the monumental task that lay ahead: the founding of an order destined to rekindle Christian faith where heresies had sown doubt and discord.

The path leading to the formation of the Order of Preachers, or Dominicans, was neither straightforward nor unchallenged. It began with Dominic's profound spiritual encounters and his determined travels. While attending the University of Palencia, he immersed himself in theological studies and the scriptures, distinguishing himself with a piercing intellect and boundless charity. A famine struck, causing Dominic to sell his cherished books, which were his most prized possessions, to feed the hungry. This act of profound compassion foreshadowed the guiding principles of his future order.

In 1203, Dominic joined Diego de Acebo, the bishop of Osma, on a diplomatic mission to Denmark. It was during this journey through Languedoc, a region rife with the dualistic Cathar heresy, that Dominic's divine purpose crystalized. Here, he witnessed communities torn apart by beliefs that challenged the very bedrock of Catholic orthodoxy. His heart ached for the souls led astray, and a fervent resolve kindled within him.

While many contemporaries would have despaired at the rampant heresies, Dominic saw a fertile ground for spiritual renewal. He engaged in earnest discussions with Cathari leaders, utilizing rigorous theological arguments and gentle persuasion. Yet, he discerned that mere intellectual debate would not suffice. The missionaries of the time often traveled in opulence, a stark contrast to the austere lifestyle of the Cathari, who lived simply and appealed to the common folk's sensibilities.

In an epiphany that would change the course of history, Dominic resolved to confront heresy through a dedicated group of preachers embodying the virtues they preached. He believed that truth coupled with humility could dismantle the allure of heretical teachings. This conviction led to the establishment of a new order, sanctioned not by mere human will, but by divine providence.

Dominic's vision was endorsed by Bishop Diego, who supported him in gathering a small group of like-minded men to commence the mission in Prouille. They founded a religious house where women who had converted from Catharism could live in safety and devotion. This nascent community became a beacon of orthodox faith and piety, setting a precedent for the Dominican mission.

The crux of the Dominican order was predicated on mendicancy—preaching and begging for sustenance—eschewing material wealth to live in gospel poverty. Dominic sought approval from Pope Innocent III, mindful that papal endorsement was crucial in legitimizing his new order. The Pope, initially cautious, dreamed of a beggar who upheld the Church with his outstretched arms, a prophetic vision that convinced him of the order's divine foundation.

The formal establishment came in 1216 when Pope Honorius III issued the Bull of Confirmation, recognizing the Order of Preachers. This pivotal moment signaled the dawn of a new era. Clad in black and white habits, the Dominican friars embarked on missions across Europe, committed to preaching, teaching, and living the gospel principles. Their presence was particularly felt in the universities of Paris and Bologna, where they played indispensable roles in shaping theological education.

Dominic's unwavering commitment to the core tenets of his order—rigorous study, persuasive preaching, and ascetic living—paved the way for its rapid expansion. The Dominicans garnered admiration and followers not through force, but through the sheer power of truth articulated with genuine humility. They became formidable opponents to heresy, their learned discourses and virtuous lives transforming skeptics into believers.

The intellectual vigor of the Dominicans birthed luminaries such as Thomas Aquinas, whose writings continue to illuminate Catholic doctrine. The friars' dedication to education extended beyond cloister walls, as they established schools and universities, fostering a culture of learning and piety. Their ceaseless efforts to combat heresies, educate clergy, and minister to the laity marked a renaissance of faith and reason in medieval Europe.

Though Dominic's own life was not prolonged—he passed from this world in 1221, aged fifty-one—the institution he founded flourished beyond his mortal span. His final resting place in Bologna became a pilgrimage site, drawing faithful hearts inspired by his legacy. Truly, Dominic Guzman's founding of the Dominicans was a divine orchestration that reshaped the spiritual landscape of Christendom, fortifying the Church against the tempests of heresy and ignorance.

In contemplating the order's foundation, we discern the intricate interplay of divine guidance and human endeavor. Dominic, driven by an unquenchable zeal for souls and the sanctity of truth, exemplified the spirit of Christ's oblation. The Dominicans, inbuilt with this spirit, have since carried forth the torch of faith, illuminating the shadows of doubt and rekindling the flame of divine love throughout history.

So it is that the founding of the Dominicans remains a testament to faith's vitality, the indomitable spirit of evangelization, and the relentless pursuit of divine truth. This chapter in the annals of the Church stands as a beacon, reminding all of the transformative power that resides in a heart wholly given to God's service.

Chapter 4: The Siege of Vienna

As dawn approached on the fateful day of September 12, 1683, the air around Vienna grew thick with the mingled tension of dread and hope. The beleaguered city's walls, scarred by months of relentless Ottoman bombardment, stood as a testament to both human resilience and frailty. Amidst the clamor of preparations and the somber prayers whispered in candlelit churches, the citizens of Vienna awaited their fate with bated breath. Yet it was within this crucible of conflict that the divine interplay of destiny and mortal valor would unfold. The strategic importance of Vienna, not merely as a bastion of Catholic Europe but as a symbol of Christendom's enduring spirit, cannot be overstated. When the gallant Polish King, John III Sobieski, surged forward with his hussars, a celestial mandate seemed to drive him. Vienna's defense was not simply an act of war; it was a sacrament of survival, a vivid tableau wherein valorous arms and devout souls coalesced to stave off the specter of conquest. Thus, the Siege of Vienna became a pivotal fulcrum in the grand narrative of civilization, where the clash of steel and the invocation of the Virgin's aid scripted a chapter that resounds throughout history.

The Strategic Importance of Vienna

Amidst the turmoil and ceaseless march of empires, Vienna emerges as a fulcrum of destiny, a citadel whose influence radiates far beyond the immediate vicinity of its formidable walls. This Austrian capital, ensconced on the banks of the Danube River, assumes a perennial significance, not only for its geographical placement but also for its political and cultural stature. At the crossroads of Europe, it channels the energies of East and West, becoming the inevitable theater of historical confrontations and theological reckonings.

The geographical importance of Vienna can hardly be overstated. Nestled within the protective enclosure of the Carpathian Mountains and strategically positioned along the Danube, Vienna serves as the gateway between Western Europe and the vast Ottoman territories to the southeast. Its location made it a linchpin in the defense against the relentless Ottoman expansion. The city, situated at a choke point along this vital waterway, thus stood as the sentinel safeguarding the pathways into the heartlands of European Christendom.

From a political standpoint, Vienna represented the Habsburg dynasty's seat of power, an essential bulwark of unity amidst the fragmented Holy Roman Empire. The Habsburgs, emboldened by their dynastic might, envisioned Vienna not only as a fortress but also as a beacon of Catholicism amidst the encroaching shadows of Islam. The city's fortified walls and grandiose architecture spoke to its dual role as both a bastion and a symbol, embodying the resilience and steadfastness of the Christian faith against formidable adversaries.

Indeed, Vienna's significance extends beyond mere martial considerations. It held within its bastions the intellectual and cultural heritage of Christendom. Universities, monastic schools, and libraries teemed with the intellectual wealth of centuries of scholarship and tradition, thereby making the city a repository of knowledge and a crucible for enlightenment. The safeguarding of Vienna was, by extension, the preservation of a collective memory and an inheritance of belief that threaded through the very essence of Western European identity.

The specter of Vienna falling into Ottoman hands would have reverberated disastrously throughout Europe. Such a calamity would not merely result in the loss of a city but engender a profound psychological and moral blow to the collective spirit of Christendom. The fortitude of Vienna mirrored the resilience of the Catholic faithful, taking a stand against the tempestuous surge of an alien creed. The city was underlined by an existential urgency: that the defense of Vienna was tantamount to the defense of Christendom itself.

The Ottoman siege of 1683 epitomized the city's enduring importance. The Habsburgs, in their diplomatic astuteness, galvanized the support of European allies, consolidating a coalition that underscored Vienna's strategic and symbolic resonance. The Polish King, John III Sobieski, answered the clarion call, reinforcing the notion that Vienna's fate was intertwined with that of the broader Christian world. Sobieski's daring intervention was not merely tactical; it was an embodiment of a cultural and spiritual crusade, sanctified by the invocation of the Virgin Mary.

Furthermore, the economic dimensions of Vienna's strategic importance deserve mention. As a bustling hub of commerce and trade, the city facilitated the flow of goods, ideas, and peoples across the European continent. The market squares buzzed with the diverse languages and wares of merchants, artisans, and traders who frequented this critical juncture. Thus, the fall of Vienna would have precipitated an economic disruption of unparalleled magnitude, severing the vital arteries upon which European prosperity depended.

In sum, Vienna, by virtue of its location, political centrality, cultural richness, and economic significance, assumed a role of unparalleled importance during the Siege of Vienna. The preservation of this city was not merely a military triumph but a testament to the indomitable spirit of the Catholic faith. It was a bulwark against the manifold threats that sought to unravel the tapestry of European Christendom. The strategic importance of Vienna stands, therefore, as a linchpin in the broader narrative of a civilization poised on the precipice, yet resolute in its convictions and unyielding in its faith.

Preparations for Defense

The twilight of summer in 1683 shrouded Vienna in a palpable tension, impregnated with the urgency of impending strife. As the Ottoman Empire's relentless march towards the heart of Europe continued unabated, the fortress city—strategically pivotal to both Christendom and the invaders—braced itself for a confrontation that would echo through the annals of history. This confrontation was not merely about the sovereignty of Vienna nor solely about defending a piece of land; it bore the latent struggle between civilizations, faiths, and the existential identity of a continent.

Vienna's defenders, suffused with a blend of stoic resolve and grim determination, recognized the unspeakable gravity of their endeavor. Habsburg Governor Count Ernst Rüdiger von Starhemberg, an indomitable figure of unyielding gallantry, steered the preparations with a hands-on approach. Under his watchful eye, the city's fortifications were scrutinized and bolstered. Ramparts were strengthened, bastions revisited, and supplies stockpiled with painstaking precision. Every stone and wooden plank of the defenses stood as a bulwark against the impending deluge, a testament to the collective will to resist and prevail.

Moreover, the intricate network of resources within Vienna itself underwent meticulous enhancement. The armories reverberated with the continuous clanging of blacksmiths' anvils as they forged new pikes, swords, and musket balls. The citizens, transcending their daily roles, metamorphosed into a cohesive force. Bakers baked incessantly to ensure bread supplies did not dwindle, while the town's butchers and farmers coordinated to sustain the defenders' nourishment.

Preparations went beyond mere physical fortifications; the emotional and spiritual armamentarium was equally paramount. The ecclesiastical influence was a binding force, infusing the populace with a sense of divine mission. The clergy, under the auspices of the Viennese Metropolitan Bishop, called for incessant prayers and fasting, invoking Our Lady's intervention and protection. These supplications were a wartime liturgy, a celestial alignment of faith and fortitude. The faithful saw their struggles mirrored in the stories of their saints; their resolve was girded by the harrowing yet triumphant tales of martyrs and crusaders.

By the late summer eve, reports burgeoned of an immense Ottoman force amassing on Vienna's periphery. The beleaguered walls seemed to bear the weight not just of anticipation but of history itself. The defenders, a motley of soldiers, civilians, and devout clerics, coalesced under the auspices of Count Starhemberg's seasoned command. Each stratagem and tactic deliberated within the Council of War was meticulously calculated, weighed against the wisdom of their forbearers and the immediacies of their perilous plight.

The Ottomans, relentless in their ambition, began peculiar movements, sending scouts and small units to test the city's external defenses. Vienna's response was swift and scrupulous; watchtowers were manned around the clock, alert for any sign of Turkish advance. Within the city, an atmosphere of quintiessential vigilance prevailed. Citizens became sentinels, contributing as auxiliary eyes and ears to predict and preempt incursions. Vienna's defenses were an impeccable mesh of professional soldiery and civilian vigilance, both underpinned by an indefatigable spirit.

The ingenuity of Vienna's commanders was exemplified by their understanding of war not merely as brute confrontation but as an interplay of tactics. Mines and countermines were an emphatic part of these preparations. To forestall the Ottoman penchant for undermining city walls, Vienna's engineers set to work digging countermines—an unseen labyrinth meant to preclude any tunneling attempts by the invaders. It was an underground cat-and-mouse game, a clandestine duel of earth and fire.

In the midst of these preparative measures, diplomatic channels were still fleetingly agog, even if under covert auspices. Emissaries frenetically communicated with allied states, beseeching for reinforcements. The glimmer of salvation arrived through coded missives indicating that the Polish King, John III Sobieski, was mobilizing his forces to aid Vienna. A beacon of hope blazed amidst the ominous clouds of war. However, no false hope was harbored; the Viennese knew well that each day of resilience was vital to delay the Ottoman full-force onslaught until reinforcements could indeed arrive.

As providence would dictate, the necessity to outlast the Ottoman siege was a saga of not just survival, but of triumphant expectancy. Count Starhemberg instilled within his men not merely the duty to fight but the acumen of patience and prudent aggression. Through unexpected sallies and nocturnal raids, the Ottomans faced piecemeal attrition— a measured frugality in battle tactics aimed at wearing down the besiegers, not by sheer power but through an obstinate resilience.

The city's medical and logistic provisions equally reflected an understanding of comprehensive war. Surgeons readied their implements, and stockpiles of medicinal herbs and remedies were accrued. Gardens within and around the city were repurposed to sustain medical needs— strips of linen were cut for bandages, and reservoirs of fresh water meticulously guarded. Consequently, the beleaguered citadel was not just a fortress but a living entity, resolutely pitted against an overwhelming force with every sinew and resource it could muster.

Thus, within the walls of Vienna, every movement echoed an unspoken pact— a covenant of endurance sworn to uphold the bastion of Christendom against the Ottoman scourge. Men and women, the clerical and the lay, soldiers and artisans—all were enshrined in the sacred purpose of their beleaguered sanctuary.

In those waning days of summer, as the first wisps of autumn began their cold descent, the defenders of Vienna stood undaunted. The magnitude of their preparations bore a composite witness to their resolve and faith. It was not just their lives or their city at peril, but the very spirit of their civilization. Each stone fortification, each whispered prayer, and each sacrificial endeavor marked their readiness for the ordeal, their solemn pledge to stand firm for the glory of Christendom. In this confluence of piety and valor, Vienna fortified its ramparts and soul, awaiting the tempest with an unyielding heart.

Chapter 5: John III Sobieski: The Catholic King

In those days of peril and unease, when the shadows of the Ottoman Crescent loomed large over the Christian realms, there arose a sovereign champion destined to be the bulwark of Christendom. John III Sobieski, King of Poland and Grand Duke of Lithuania, was a figure whose early life bore the seeds of his future grandeur. Raised amidst the chivalric traditions of his time and deeply devout in his Catholic faith, Sobieski's reign was marked by an ardent reverence for the Blessed Virgin Mary. His victories, particularly the monumental relief of Vienna, were not merely triumphs of military strategy but acts suffused with religious zeal. He knelt in prayer before going into battle, invoking Mary's protection, and it is said that this reliance on divine intercession galvanized his troops, infusing them with unshakable resolve. Sobieski's contributions were not confined to the battlefield; they resonated through the annals of civilization itself, fortifying the moral and cultural foundations of a Europe poised at the crossroads of destiny.

Early Life and Reign of Sobieski

Emerging from the humble yet illustrious lands of the Polish-Lithuanian Commonwealth, John III Sobieski entered this world on August 17, 1629, in Olesko Castle. Sobieski's early years bore the imprint of an era steeped in political turbulence and relentless warfare. Born into the noble Sobieski family, young John was nourished on tales of chivalry and devotion, cultivating an early fascination with the martial and religious fervor that would later define his reign.

Sobieski hailed from a venerable lineage, the Sobieskis being venerated as exemplars of patriotic virtue and military valor. His father, Jakub Sobieski, was a prominent castellany and military commander, while his mother, Zofia Teofillia, infused in him a stoic yet fervent devotion to the Catholic faith. As an heir to such a storied legacy, John's upbringing was steeped in the twin pursuits of erudition and knightly discipline.

Educated in a Jesuit college in Krakow, Sobieski immersed himself in the classical canons of philosophy and literature, ascending the rungs of intellectual enlightenment. His sojourn abroad, particularly in France, exposed him to the shiftingly intricate chessboard of European politics. Sobieski's education, far from merely academic, was an essential crucible that shaped his diplomatic acumen and his nuanced understanding of the manifold threats Europe faced. By his early twenties, Sobieski had forged a formidable presence, deftly balancing the erudition of a scholar with the prowess of a warrior.

The mid-seventeenth century saw the Polish-Lithuanian Commonwealth besieged by internal strife and external incursions. The tempestuous Khmelnytsky Uprising and the Deluge, an extensive series of wars and invasions, had left the Commonwealth beleaguered. In this crucible of chaos, Sobieski's ascent was inexorable. Earning his stripes in the harrowing battles against the Cossacks and Swedes, he demonstrated feats of gallantry and tactical brilliance that riveted the gaze of his contemporaries and positioned him as a beacon of hope.

In the year 1674, Sobieski's ascension to the throne was not merely a coronation; it was the consummation of divine providence and national yearning. His election as the King of Poland and Grand Duke of Lithuania transpired during an epoch fraught with existential peril. The Ottoman Empire, with its insatiable ambitions, cast its menacing shadow over Christendom, threatening the religious and cultural sanctity of Europe. To the Commonwealth, Sobieski was not merely a monarch; he was a bulwark against the encroaching tide of tyranny.

Upon assuming the mantle of kingship, Sobieski's reign was infused with a profound devotion to the Virgin Mary. This devotion was not a mere personal piety but a salient element of his political ethos. The consecration of his military campaigns and victories to Mary symbolized a relentless crusade to fortify the bastions of Christendom against the Ottoman onslaught. With a fervor reminiscent of the ancient paladins, Sobieski sought to encapsulate his kingdom within the aegis of divine protection.

Sobieski's rule was characterized by an amalgam of military might and shrewd statesmanship. His reign fortified the Commonwealth's defenses through a series of military reforms and diplomatic alliances, which were instrumental in stabilizing the region. His diplomatic acumen was particularly evident in forging a network of alliances, reaffirming the Commonwealth's position as a pivotal bulwark against the crescent's expansion. By deftly navigating the labyrinthine corridors of European diplomacy, he ensured that the Commonwealth remained a linchpin in the continental balance of power.

Under Sobieski's leadership, the Polish-Lithuanian Commonwealth evolved from a state beleaguered by fractious nobility and external threats to a unified entity capable of withstanding adversaries. His military campaigns against Tatars and Turks demonstrated a sophisticated grasp of tactical innovation, often leveraging terrain, timing, and logistical prowess to outmaneuver and outflank enemy forces. These campaigns were undergirded by a singular vision – to sustain, if not expand, the bastions of Christianity against the infidel's unholy advance.

Sobieski's devoutness to the Virgin Mary and the ebbing, flowing tides of his godly devotion permeated not only his military endeavors but also his governance. Through ecclesiastical patronage, he facilitated the construction and endowment of numerous churches and monastic institutions. His reign also saw the compilation of theological treatises and the flourishing of religious art, imbuing the Commonwealth with a radiant tapestry of the Catholic faith and an enduring testament to Sobieski's piety.

Yet, it was upon the fertile fields of Vienna that Sobieski's most profound and indelible legacy would be etched. The Siege of Vienna in 1683 represented not only the apogee of Sobieski's martial prowess but also his enduring contribution to Christendom. In a dramatic maneuver, Sobieski, at the helm of the Holy League, orchestrated what would become a seminal victory over the Ottomans. This triumph, consecrated in the name of the Virgin Mary, was a fervent affirmation of the indomitable spirit of Christendom and the providential righteousness of Sobieski's reign.

In the annals of history, John III Sobieski emerges as a paragon of faith and fortitude, a king whose early life and reign were inexorably entwined with the sacrosanct mission to defend and perpetuate the Catholic faith. His victories, underscored by devout Marian devotion, not only secured his realm but also resounded through the corridors of civilization, sending ripples across the fabric of Christendom. Thus, Sobieski's reign stands as a testament to the enduring power of faith and the celestial triumph of righteousness over tyranny.

Sobieski's Devotion to Mary

As the drums of war echoed through Poland and the specter of Ottoman conquest loomed large, King John III Sobieski turned to a source of strength and guidance that had been his steadfast companion throughout his life. From his early years to the height of his reign, Sobieski's devotion to the Blessed Virgin Mary was unyielding, imbuing his every decision with a sense of divine purpose and fortitude. In seeking the intercession of the Mother of God, Sobieski found not just solace, but a fervent inspiration that would guide him through the trials that lay ahead.

Mary's influence on Sobieski was more than mere personal piety; it was a binding covenant that shaped his reign and his resolve. The Polish king regarded Marian devotion as a cornerstone of his spiritual and temporal endeavors. As he prepared to lead his troops into battle against the formidable forces of the Ottoman Empire, Sobieski did so with the firm belief that he was an instrument of Divine Providence, selected by Mary herself to defend Christendom from encroaching threats.

This unwavering devotion manifested itself in various ways, from the grand to the intimate. One notable reflection of his Marian devotion was the inclusion of the Blessed Virgin's image on his battle standards and personal arms. These were no mere decorations; they were powerful symbols of his trust in Mary's protection and advocacy. His troops, emboldened by their sovereign's faith, embraced these symbols with a similar fervent hope, believing that their cause had divine endorsement and guidance.

Sobieski's prayers to Mary were heartfelt and frequent, forming an essential part of his daily life. He would often retreat to his private chapel to seek her intercession, particularly before making crucial decisions or engaging in significant battles. These moments of solitude and prayer became his sanctuary, where he found the spiritual fortitude necessary to lead his nation. In Mary's name, alliances were sought and battles were fought, with the Polish king ever trusting in her heavenly guidance.

During the arduous march to Vienna, Sobieski's devotion was a beacon that rallied his weary troops. The soldiers, facing exhaustion and the ever-present threat of ambush, were constantly reminded of their king's unwavering faith. Sobieski's generals and soldiers alike found solace in his conviction, and Marian hymns became a source of communal strength and comfort during the grueling journey. The invocation of Mary served not merely as a spiritual exercise but as a unifying force that fortified their resolve.

In September of 1683, as the opposing armies prepared for the Siege of Vienna, Sobieski prayed fervently for Mary's intercession. He led his army in a mass, dedicating their cause and their lives to the Blessed Virgin. This solemn act of consecration reflected not only Sobieski's personal devotion but also his strategic understanding that the morale of his troops was intertwined with their faith. His army, convinced that they fought under the protection of the heavenly Queen, marched into battle with a boldness and confidence that transcended human limitations.

As the battle unfolded, Sobieski's faith did not waver. In the thick of combat, amidst the chaos and clamor of war, his prayers ascended to the heavens. It is said that in the climactic moments of the battle, he invoked Mary's name, urging his soldiers to fight with valor for the glory of God and the honor of the Mother of Christ. The fervor with which they fought bore testament to a deeply ingrained belief that they were part of a divine mission.

Following the decisive victory at Vienna, Sobieski's first act was one of thanksgiving. He visited a nearby chapel dedicated to the Virgin Mary, offering prayers of gratitude for her intercession. This act of deep humility and reverence was more than a personal gesture; it was a proclamation of faith to all of Christendom. Sobieski's victory was hailed as a triumph not just of military strategy, but of divine intervention and Marian devotion.

Sobieski's reverence for Mary extended beyond the battlefield. He was instrumental in promoting Marian devotion throughout Poland, encouraging the construction of Marian shrines and the celebration of her feasts with grand solemnity. Under his reign, Poland flourished as a bastion of Marian piety, with countless dedications made to the Blessed Virgin. These acts reinforced the spiritual fabric of the nation, creating a legacy of devotion that outlived the reign of the Catholic king.

Moreover, Sobieski fostered a connection between the Polish crown and the Holy See, aligning his kingdom's spiritual and political aspirations with the broader goals of Christendom. His devotion to Mary was a critical element in this alignment, as it symbolized the unity of purpose between the Polish nation and the Catholic Church. The Pope himself recognized and commended Sobieski's faith, further solidifying his role as a champion of the Catholic cause.

In summary, John III Sobieski's devotion to the Blessed Virgin Mary was not merely a personal faith but a public testament to the power of divine intercession. It shaped his leadership, reinforced his troops' morale, and cemented his legacy as the noble defender of Christendom. Through Mary's intercession, Sobieski was empowered to lead with grace, courage, and unwavering conviction, ensuring that his contributions to civilization and the Catholic faith would be remembered for generations.

Chapter 6: The March to Vienna

Drawn by divine purpose and led by their unwavering faith, John III Sobieski and his valiant Polish forces commenced their arduous march to Vienna with all the haste and fervor of a crusade. The king's clarion call echoed through the land, assembling a host whose resolve mirrored that of ancient warriors defending Christendom against an encroaching darkness. The journey was fraught with trials, where every step was a testament to human endurance and logistical prowess, navigating treacherous terrain without respite. Yet, lingering in their hearts was a beacon of hope, a shared conviction that they were but instruments in the hands of Providence. As they pressed on, the celestial intercession of the Blessed Virgin seemed to guide their path, emboldening their spirits despite the ceaseless adversity. In the annals of history, their march stands immortal, a testament to the sacrifice and unity that would soon alter the fate of Europe forever.

Hasty Mobilization from Poland

In the annals of Christendom, the swift and decisive mobilization from Poland stands as a testament to the fortitude and piety of the Polish forces, led by the indomitable King John III Sobieski. This chapter in our collective history is not merely a recounting of military logistics; it is an ode to the holy zeal and undying faith that propelled an army towards what seemed an insurmountable endeavor.

The hour was dire. With the Ottoman Empire advancing upon Vienna, the capital of the Habsburg Monarchy, Europe trembled at the prospect of succumbing to the crescent. Letters of desperation flew to the courts of Christendom, imploring for succor against this mighty foe. Among these missives, the plea from Emperor Leopold I reached the ears of King Sobieski, a monarch whose heart was ever ardent for the cause of the Virgin Mary and the defense of Christian realms.

Sobieski knew well that time was not an ally. The siege of Vienna had tightened its noose, and the city groaned under the weight of its besiegers. There was no luxury of prolonged preparation or the measured gathering of forces. The King issued a clarion call to arms, summoning his knights and soldiers with an expeditious urgency that allowed no room for hesitation. The response was swift, yet imbued with a sense of destiny; for who could deny that it was providence guiding these men to save the heart of Europe?

The Polish forces, though seasoned and battle-hardened, faced an arduous journey. From Kraków to Vienna lay hundreds of miles replete with treacherous terrain, perilous rivers, and the ever-looming specter of ambush by roving Ottoman scouts. The hastily assembled battalions comprised not only men-at-arms but also civilians, wagoners, and even clergy, all united under Sobieski's banner. What bound them together with such unyielding resolve was a shared conviction—the belief that they marched not merely to aid a besieged city but to uphold the divine order willed by Almighty God.

As word of Sobieski's mobilization spread, it infused both allies and adversaries with a profound sense of anticipation. For the Austrians and their European compatriots, this movement of troops promised not merely a reinforcement but a salvation. For the Ottomans, it signified the stirring of a formidable behemoth they would be wise not to underestimate. Yet, it was more than just military might that Sobieski brought forth; his columns were animated by a fervent spiritual resolve, as they bore with them the icon of Our Lady of Częstochowa, the Black Madonna, a sacred emblem around which the soldiers rallied.

The march was relentless. Days blurred into nights as the army pressed forward with tireless vigor. Provisions were scarce, and fatigue gnawed at the heels of even the most stalwart soldiers, yet they persisted. Sobieski's leadership was as much about sustaining morale as it was about tactical acumen. He often joined his men in prayer, invoking the intercession of the Blessed Mother to guide and protect them. His presence among them was an anchor, instilling a deep-rooted belief that their cause was righteous and that victory, though daunting, was attainable.

It is worth noting the logistical feats accomplished during this hasty mobilization. The lines of communication and supply were kept remarkably intact despite the speed of advance. Scouts and outriders ensured the main body of the army could move with strategic coherence, avoiding potential pitfalls and setting up necessary waystations where exhausted troops could find brief respite. This meticulous coordination was crucial in ensuring that Sobieski's forces arrived not as a ragged assembly but as a disciplined, battle-ready contingent.

Sobieski's march to Vienna was marked by numerous skirmishes and minor engagements. These encounters, though not decisive in isolation, served to sharpen the resolve and hone the fighting prowess of his men. The Poles, renowned cavalrymen, especially the famed winged hussars, found their spirits emboldened by these conflicts. They became even more convinced that they carried the mantle of God's warriors, destined to break the siege and repel the invaders.

As they neared the plains of Vienna, the gravity of their mission weighed heavily upon them. This was not merely a battle for territory but a struggle for the spiritual and cultural survival of Christendom. It was in this profound realization that Sobieski found his greatest strength as a leader. He reminded his forces that their fight was a sacred duty, consecrated by their unwavering devotion to the Virgin Mary and the sanctity of their Christian faith.

What must have transpired in the minds of those soldiers, as they glimpsed the embattled city walls of Vienna on the horizon? Standing on the cusp of destiny, they knew that the fate of Europe hung in the balance. The march, fraught with peril and perseverance, was but a prelude to the great confrontation that would follow. Yet, in their hearts burned a fierce confidence—they were no mere mercenaries or adventurers, but the chosen instruments of divine will, led by a King who embodied the virtues of courage, faith, and divine devotion.

Thus, the hasty mobilization from Poland signifies more than a remarkable feat of military preparedness. It stands as a vivid illustration of a people united in purpose, driven by an unwavering belief in their sacred mission. The convergence of strategic acumen, spiritual fervor, and the indomitable will of a pious king created a force that would alter the course of history. As they prepared to join the fateful battle for Vienna, the Polish forces carried with them not just weapons of war, but the hopes and prayers of a continent. They marched under the mantle of Mary, guided by a conviction that their cause was just and their victory, as yet unearned, divinely assured.

And so, the stage was set, the players in position, and the first act of this monumental drama drew to a close. What would unfold in the shadow of Vienna's walls would be nothing short of extraordinary, a testament to faith, valor, and the enduring spirit of Christendom.

Logistics and Challenges of the Forced March

The journey from the Kingdom of Poland to Vienna was neither simple nor straightforward. This arduous trek began as a hasty mobilization, with the Polish forces mustering on short notice, propelled by the urgent need to aid their fellow Christians and defend Vienna from the Ottoman menace. The logistical web woven to ensure the army's capacity for this immense task was intricate and replete with obstacles. Not merely a challenge of distance, the march encompassed the trepidations of terrain, supply shortages, and the continual threat of engagement with hostile forces.

Commencement of the march was already a feat. King John III Sobieski, beloved by his men, inspired a resolute determination among his troops. Yet, motivation did not suffice to surmount the tangible barriers which stood in their path. Sobieski himself, a seasoned strategist, knew well that the success of any operation lay in the unseen gears of logistics. From securing sufficient provisions to ensuring the health and morale of his men, every aspect demanded meticulous orchestration.

Considering the sheer distance traversed – nearly 600 miles through the rugged terrains of the Carpathians and across the fertile, but uncertain plains of Hungary – the undertaking was monumental. Each step of the journey posed its own set of trials. The mountainous paths, though picturesque, proved hostile to an army laden with weaponry and baggage. Narrow trails, often slick with mud from summer rains, risked the misfortune of lost traction, potentially costing lives or vital supplies. Conversely, the expansive plains, though devoid of such topographical hindrances, left the troops exposed to the elements and potential ambuscades from Ottoman scouts.

This march was not a parade of triumph; it was a calculated gamble against time. Provisions were a point of continual concern. Initial supplies stockpiled from Polish granaries and foraged from local townships were soon depleted, forcing the army into a precarious reliance on foraging and requisition from allied territories. The ever-present specter of starvation loomed, with rationing becoming stricter with each passing day. Sobieski's leadership reflected an acute awareness of this delicate balance, where each decision could tip the scales between sustenance and destitution.

Beyond mere physical supplies, the march necessitated an intricate command of morale. The soldiers, driven by a combination of faith and duty, required fortification not only in body but in spirit. The weight of the Marian devotion, the symbol of the Lady of Czestochowa, remained central in keeping the fervor ablaze within their breasts. Regular prayers, hymns, and the presence of priests provided a modicum of comfort amidst the trials, creating a sanctuary of faith within the heart of each soldier that transcended the corporeal struggles they faced.

The threat of disease was another relentless adversary, inscrutable and indiscriminate. The confines of close quarters and the stress of continuous movement fostered a breeding ground for afflictions. Dysentery, fevers, and other maladies struck without regard, sapping the vitality of men faster than any blade might. Medics, working with rudimentary means, faced the daunting task of containing outbreaks, administering what meager remedies they could procure or concoct from the wild herbs and alchemical knowledge of the day.

Communication presented another daunting hurdle. In an age predating the convenience of modern telecommunications, reliance on couriers was paramount. Messages bearing critical tactical updates had to traverse the unmapped, oft-hostile landscapes at a speed dictated by the endurance of horse and rider. Coordination with allied forces, such as the Imperial troops of the Holy Roman Empire, required a synchrony of movement and strategy that tested the limits of their methodologies. Delays or miscommunications bore the potential for catastrophic disarray.

Furthermore, the terrain was not merely a passive backdrop but a dynamic component influencing the tactical considerations. Valleys and forests provided not just aesthetic relief but strategic advantages or liabilities. The need to ascertain and navigate through the avoidant routes unseen by enemy scouts, often dictated sudden and unanticipated alterations in their course. This constant re-calibration tested the resolve and adaptability of the both men and their commanders.

The wear on the men and beasts of burden requires no understatement. Horses, as the prime movers of both knights and supply carts, endured relentless strain. The fatigue on these noble creatures mirrored that of their human counterparts. Spare mounts, meant to replace the debilitated, dwindled as the march progressed, making the conservation and care of existing stock pivotal. Stables erected in brief halts became triage centers, where farriers and veterinarians worked tirelessly to maintain the lifeblood of the army's mobility.

Adding to these natural impediments were the psychological trials faced by the marching army. The specter of the Ottoman force, an ever-present mental gauntlet, hung over their spirits like an encroaching storm. Rumors and intelligence reports of the Ottoman numbers and prowess varied, sowing seeds of unease. Sobieski's ability to maintain morale in such a climate was a testament to his charismatic leadership, his speeches acting as balm to the anxieties swirling through the ranks.

On several occasions, the force had to contend with skirmishes against forward Ottoman units. These encounters, though minor compared to the coming storm at Vienna, chipped away at the strength and supplies of the Polish force. Yet, each victory in these minor engagements served to bolster their confidence and whet their readiness for the larger conflict looming on the horizon.

Another logistical quandary was the management of alliances and coordination with the Holy Roman Empire's forces. Navigating the labyrinthine politics of the time, ensuring that mutual respect and cooperation prevailed over distrust and hesitation, demanded astute diplomacy. The precariousness of such alliances meant that any lapse in communication or perceived slight could unravel the solidarity so essential for the upcoming confrontation with the Ottoman host.

When the army finally neared Vienna, with Sobieski at its lead, wearied from the journey but resolute, the culmination of their relentless march stood as a testament to human endurance and the unyielding spirit driven by faith and duty. The logistical mastery exhibited in getting an army across such treacherous expanses unto the gates of Vienna was not merely an appendix to their valor but was integral to the very framework of their impending victory.

The forced march to Vienna epitomized a confluence of faith-inspired determination, rigorous strategic planning, and a willingness to endure profoundly harsh conditions. Such efforts were not merely the grim backdrop of glory but were indispensable to the defense of Christendom. This logistical prowess, grounded in careful foresight and adaptability to the ever-shifting circumstances, ensured that Sobieski's forces arrived not as a ragged assembly but as a disciplined and fervent force ready to turn the tide of history.

Thus, as we reflect upon the eventual triumph that graced Vienna, and by extension Christendom, it becomes unequivocally clear that the march - with all its trials, tribulations, and triumphs - was a crucible that forged not just warriors, but heroes of unwavering faith and resolve.

Chapter 7: The Feast of Our Lady's Assumption

On the 15th of August, known reverently as the Feast of Our Lady's Assumption, all of Christendom seemed to hold its breath, suspended between the earthly strife of man and the celestial promise of divine intervention. The majestic bells tolled with a resonance that pierced the hearts and minds of soldiers and civilians alike, lifting their spirits high amidst the dense fog of war. It was not merely a feast but a herald of hope, an echo of Mary's grace that burgeoned within each faithful heart. Poland's king, Jan Sobieski, found his resolve fortified by such sacred moments, drawing upon the unwavering belief that their struggles were sanctified by the Mother of God herself. As the legions gathered, the blessed day steered their will with an orchestrated harmony, intertwining their piety and valor. The religious fervor overcast the strategic realm, blending it into a singular purpose—triumph not just over flesh and blood, but a spiritual conquest sanctified by Marian devotion. Imbued with the solemnity of this holy feast, Sobieski's campaign was no longer a series of maneuvers but a divine mission, one that would aim to etch their undying faith into the annals of history.

The Feast of Our Lady's Assumption

The Feast of Our Lady's Assumption, observed with profound reverence by Roman Catholics around the globe, occupies a paramount position not just for its religious solemnity but for its resonance in the annals of Christendom. This sacred day, dedicated to the Virgin Mary's ascension to Heaven, intertwines divinely with moments of monumental historical significance, particularly during the Siege of Vienna in 1683. The religious import of this feast is multifaceted, touching upon theological doctrines, ecclesiastical traditions, and historical victories that, to the faithful, bear the indelible mark of divine intervention.

In the Catholic tradition, the Assumption of Mary holds that the Mother of God was assumed body and soul into heavenly glory at the end of her earthly life. This dogma, solemnly promulgated by Pope Pius XII in the apostolic constitution "Munificentissimus Deus" in 1950, drew from centuries of veneration and belief within the Church. The roots of this conviction, however, extend far deeper into the early centuries of Christianity, anchored in both the apocryphal "Transitus Mariae" texts and the teachings of early Church Fathers. It is within this rich theological tapestry that the Feast of Our Lady's Assumption was celebrated in Europe during the late 17th century.

The celebration of the Assumption is more than a mere liturgical observance; it is a spiritual call to reflect on the celestial destiny that awaits those faithful to God's graces. The Virgin Mary, revered for her purity and obedience, becomes a symbol of hope and salvation, guiding believers through the trials of life towards the promise of eternal life. This feast, positioned at the heart of the Catholic liturgical calendar, thereby serves as both a commemoration and an inspiration, reinforcing the ultimate triumph of good over evil.

Within the context of the Siege of Vienna, the Assumption carried an exceptional significance. As John III Sobieski and his formidable army approached Vienna in September of 1683, the morale of the defenders and the besiegers alike was significantly influenced by this Marian feast. In a theater where the clash of civilizations threatened to upend the balance of power in Europe, the Assumption served as a spiritual rallying point. For Catholics, the feast articulated a divine protection and intercession that they fervently believed would manifest in the unfolding battle.

The conviction of divine favor was no mere abstraction. It materialized palpably in the resolve and ingenuity demonstrated by Sobieski and his troops. The siege, which had placed Vienna on the precipice of despair, was lifted miraculously on the very day dedicated to Our Lady. Such synchronicity of events was scarcely viewed as fortuitous by the faithful; rather, it was interpreted as a clear sign of the Heavenly aid invoked through devotion to Mary. It reified the belief that the Blessed Virgin's intercession was not only a cornerstone of personal piety but a shield for Christendom itself.

The spiritual preparations of the troops, alongside the physical ones, are worthy of note. Camp altars became the nuclei of fervent prayers, and the Holy Sacraments were frequently administered. The Marian hymns, resounding through the encampments under starry skies, imbued the soldiers and commanding officers with a sense of divine mission. It was as if the ethereal presence of the Blessed Virgin pervaded the very atmosphere, lending courage and fortitude where despondency might otherwise have prevailed. This palpable sense of maternal protection and heavenly favor framed the events of that blessed day in a sacred narrative of divine deliverance.

In the aftermath of the battle, Sobieski's devotion to Mary was heralded as a testament to the power of faith in the recounting of this monumental victory. The victory at Vienna was not merely a triumph of military strategy but a divine vindication of Marian intercession. Thus, Our Lady's Assumption came to symbolize not only the ascent of Mary herself but also the ascent of Christian forces over the adversary of that era. The resonance of this victory, resonant with Marian devotion, would echo through the corridors of power and faith, reinforcing the sanctity of the Feast.

The theological implications of this Marian feast were further accentuated by the eventual proclamation of the Assumption as dogma. The victory over the Imams at Vienna, seen as a reflection of the Church's struggle against heresy and non-Christian forces, took on an eschatological dimension. The Assumption represented the paradigmatic victory of purity, grace, and divine intervention over all forms of evil and opposition. It reaffirmed the Catholic doctrine of Mary's unique role in the salvific plan, underscoring the Church's mission to resist the encroachments of secular and non-Christian powers.

Moreover, the spiritual significance of the Assumption extended beyond the realm of battlefields and into the hearts of the common faithful. It reinforced the belief in Mary's perpetual intercession, nurturing devotion and leading to the establishment of innumerable confraternities and sodalities dedicated to her. This Marian devotion became a wellspring of spiritual strength and a source of communal identity for Catholics, embodying the peaceful yet potent resistance against moral and spiritual decay.

The liturgical celebrations surrounding the Feast of the Assumption continue to evoke the poignant memory of Vienna's deliverance. Each year, as Catholics gather to honor the Virgin Mary, the intertwining of historical victory and religious significance reminds them of the ever-present possibility of grace and hope. Processions, masses, and prayers on this day become an act of collective remembrance, forging a continuity between the past triumphs and present faith.

In essence, the religious significance of the Feast of Our Lady's Assumption transcends its liturgical boundaries. It encapsulates the theological, historical, and spiritual dimensions that have shaped the identity of Christendom. Through the lens of Sobieski's triumph, the feast emerges as more than a mere recollection of Mary's Assumption; it stands as a testament to the enduring power of faith, intercession, and divine providence. For the devout soldiers at Vienna and the generations of believers that followed, the Assumption remains a beacon of celestial hope and a potent reminder of God's unwavering support for His faithful.

In concluding this meditation on the Feast of Our Lady's Assumption, it is clear that the day's significance permeates the very fabric of Catholic life. Mary's Assumption, intertwined with the historical victory at Vienna, serves not only as a theological affirmation but as an enduring narrative of divine intervention. It inspires reverence and devotion, while simultaneously invoking the collective memory of God's providential guidance in history. Thus, the Feast of Our Lady's Assumption continues to shine as both a religious and historical lodestar, guiding the faithful on their spiritual journey.

Influence on Morale and Strategy

On that sacred day, August 15th, the Feast of Our Lady's Assumption, much more than religious observance stirred the hearts of men. As the sun cast its golden rays over the besieged city of Vienna, a profound sense of both spiritual and martial purpose pervaded the ranks. The soldiers felt a saintly kinship with their divine protector, the Blessed Virgin Mary, whose assumed presence they believed watched over them. The Feast, a celebration of Mary's ascent to Heaven, imbued the Christian forces with an almost otherworldly vigor.

Fusing the fervor of faith with the strategy of battle, the Christian commanders recognized that this solemn feast offered more than spiritual nourishment; it was a wellspring of morale. Armed with both steel and prayer, the soldiers approached the forthcoming struggle with the Ottomans with renewed zeal. The collective psyche of the army, bathed in divine assurance, stood as impregnable as the city walls they swore to defend. Sobieski, a devout adherent of Marian devotion, deemed this feast a divine augury, interpreting the Heavenly signs as a celestial endorsement of their cause.

The significance of the Feast of Our Lady's Assumption cannot be overstated when evaluating the morale of Sobieski's troops. From grizzled veterans to fresh-faced youths, every soldier's spirit was lifted. This holy day transformed their outlook, altering the mundane rigors of war into an epic quest sanctified by divine blessing. In the eyes of the faithful, the Queen of Heaven herself had donned their colors, leading them as they prepared to confront their formidable adversaries. Their sense of righteous mission galvanized the troops, turning doubts into certainties and fears into the courageous resolve.

Strategically, the timing of the Feast offered a unique advantage. The Christian forces, observing the holy day with high solemnity, leveraged their unity to fortify their positions and plan their maneuvers. Sobieski, combining his military genius with his unwavering faith, orchestrated his troops with a masterful blend of heavenly inspiration and earthly cunning.

Commanders convened amidst the sacred verses of the Mass, ensuring every tactical decision resonated with spiritual approval. This divine endorsement became a cornerstone of their strategy, fusing religious fervor with military precision.

Moreover, the celebration emboldened not only the Christian soldiers but also the besieged citizens of Vienna. Knowing that their defenders were blessed by heavenly providence inspired the townsfolk to support the cause with heartening resilience. Supplies were procured, fortifications renewed, and a communal spirit of invincibility enveloped the city. The Feast served as a beacon of hope, illuminating the path to victory amidst the shadowy threats of the Ottoman siege.

It was amid this sacred context that Sobieski delivered his stirring pre-battle oration. No mere speech, but a heartfelt invocation, intertwining the themes of divine intercession and patriotic duty. "We fight," declared Sobieski, "under the banner of Our Lady, with Heaven as our fortress." His words resonated deeply, echoing through the ranks, solidifying their resolve. The king's unwavering devotion to Mary was palpable, his faith an anchor in the tempest of war. His leadership, both pious and pragmatic, transformed the Feast into a tactical fulcrum upon which the balance of power teetered.

The juxtaposition of the sacred and the strategic found its zenith in Sobieski's directive to emblazon Marian symbols upon their standards and armor. Thus, every soldier marched forward enshrined in emblematic sanctity, transforming the battlefield into a living tapestry of faith. This vivid display resonated deeply within the hearts of Christian warriors, searing the divine mandate into their very souls. In the clash of arms, amid the tumult and fury of battle, these holy relics served as potent reminders that their cause was just, their victory preordained by divine will.

Furthermore, the psychological impact upon the Ottoman forces cannot be diminished. Among their ranks, tales of Christian fervor and Marian zeal spread like wildfire. The sight of Sobieski's Marian-emblazoned battalions must have shaken their resolve, sowing seeds of doubt where once resided unyielding confidence. The juxtaposition of the Christian holy day against their own impending doom was not lost on the Ottoman command. To them, the Feast signified an imperceptible yet palpable shift in the celestial scales of war.

Throughout Christian history, the Feast of Our Lady's Assumption had been celebrated with reverent joy, but never had it borne such profound military significance. The Assumption, a divine mystery, infused the temporal struggle with an eternal perspective, reminding every soldier that their sacrifice on earth mirrored a greater celestial battle. Each sword swung in defense of Vienna was tempered in the fires of faith, each battle cry harmonized with the celestial hymns of angelic hosts.

As they advanced, emboldened by the patronage of Mary, the Christian soldiers perceived their struggle as a sacred duty, transcending mere earthly conflict. They were not just defenders of Vienna; they were defenders of Christendom itself. This theological underpinning elevated their mission, imbuing even the smallest skirmishes with eternal significance. The Feast functioned akin to a divine bulwark, an impenetrable shield of faith that no Ottoman sword could pierce.

In the orchestration of their strategies, the Christian commanders deftly wove the spiritual significance of the Feast into every aspect of their tactics. Troop deployments, fortifications, and battle plans mirrored a divine choreography, one in which each movement was sanctified by Mary's assumed presence. The ecclesiastical ceremonies, interweaving prayer and sacrament with martial preparations, offered a sanctuary of divine tranquility amidst the chaos. The Feast was, in every sense, the linchpin of their strategic mindset, a celestial compass guiding them towards victory.

In conclusion, the Feast of Our Lady's Assumption bestowed upon the Christian forces a dual arsenal of morale and strategy. It transformed the ordinary into the extraordinary, the mundane into the miraculous. Through Sobieski's leadership, imbued with unwavering Marian devotion, the Christian forces advanced not merely as soldiers but as holy warriors, sanctified in their quest. Indeed, on that day, the Feast didn't merely signify a liturgical celebration; it became the very soul of their martial enterprise, an indelible testament to the power of faith to shape the annals of history.

Chapter 8: The Battle Begins

The clarion of war echoed through the valleys, as the Ottomans, under the banner of the Crescent, surged with relentless might towards the gates of Vienna. Sobieski, with the grace of divine providence and the weight of kingly duty, orchestrated his forces in a display of unmatched tactical brilliance. His cavalry, the winged hussars, emerged as angels of retribution, their righteous fury echoing across the battlefield. With every clash of steel and cry of valor, it became evident that this confrontation was not merely one of men and arms but of civilizations and faiths. As dawn broke through the cannons' smoke, a new chapter for Christendom was being writ in the blood of saints and soldiers, marking the beginning of a battle that would forever alter the course of history.

The Initial Ottoman Assault

As the dawn cast its first light on the battlements of Vienna, the ominous silence that hung heavy over the city was shattered by the thunderous roar of the Ottoman cannons. The siege, having dragged on for weeks, had eroded the hope of the beleaguered defenders. Within the Ottoman camp, the sense of an imminent conquest pervaded the air, bolstered by the elaborate stratagems of their vizier, Kara Mustafa Pasha.

With disciplined precision, the Ottoman forces, a motley but formidable assembly of Janissaries, Sipahis, and irregular troops, advanced towards the city walls. The earth trembled under the onslaught of their sappers who, proficient in the art of siege warfare, dug ever closer to the city's defenses. These tireless efforts were punctuated by the relentless bombardment, a calculated endeavor to breach the fortifications and break the spirit of the defenders within.

The resolute Viennese, however, were not to be underestimated. Though vastly outnumbered, their resolve was steeled by the specter of subjugation and the bastion of their faith. Under the leadership of Count Ernst Rüdiger von Starhemberg, they marshaled every resource at their disposal, employing last-ditch measures to fortify the crumbling walls and patch the breaches as quickly as they emerged. Starhemberg's indefatigable courage served as a beacon of hope within the walls of the city, where both soldiers and citizens alike toiled day and night, driven by a collective will to resist.

Amidst this maelstrom, Victor Amadeus, Duke of Savoy, and Prince Eugene of Savoy orchestrated sorties that disrupted the Ottoman lines, creating slender windows of respite for the embattled garrison. These forays, albeit costly, were crucial in maintaining the pressure on the Ottoman besiegers and slowing their advance. Yet, the severity of the situation left the Habsburg defenders acutely aware that without timely relief, their stalwart resistance would inevitably falter.

In the surreal twilight of what seemed an endless siege, the spiritual dimension of the conflict loomed large. The piety of the Viennese defenders found its expression through fervent prayers and masses, invoking the intercession of the Blessed Virgin Mary. The churches, though battered, served as sanctuaries of solace and defiance. It was in these hallowed spaces that the seeds of hope were sown, nurturing a belief that divine intervention would come to their aid.

The relentless advance of the Ottomans reached its apogee with a coordinated assault that sought to deliver the coup de grâce to Vienna. Kara Mustafa Pasha, envisioning the city as the ultimate prize in his campaign to extend Ottoman dominion into the heart of Europe, deployed his elite Janissaries for a decisive strike. With terrifying swiftness, the Ottoman forces surged forward, their war cries mingling with the acrid smoke of musket and cannon fire.

In the ensuing chaos, the defenders faced their darkest hour. Sections of the city walls crumbled under the unyielding pressure; breaches widened, threatening to allow an influx of Ottoman troops. Yet, in this crucible of desperation, human tenacity and ingenuity shone forth brightly. Fragile yet unyielding, the defenders repelled wave after wave of assaults with a blend of strategy, valor, and indomitable spirit.

Farther afield, the cavalry of the Holy League was organizing under the auspices of divine providence and King John III Sobieski of Poland. News of the formidable Polish King's advance reached the fatigued ears of Vienna's defenders like a clarion call. Sobieski, a paragon of chivalry and ardent devotion to the Blessed Virgin, marshaled his forces with alacrity. As the banners emblazoned with the image of Mary fluttered in the wind, the combined disparate armies of the Holy League were bound by a singular purpose: to lift the siege and restore Christendom's bulwark.

The day's light lingered with an unnatural duration, an eternal twilight filled with the cacophony of war. The Ottoman siege engines, monstrous contrivances of destruction, seemed to stretch the boundaries of human endurance. Yet the Viennese defenders, who had sacrificed and bled, who had prayed and hoped ceaselessly, managed to hold their lines against the encroaching tide. Their determination was now emboldened by the anticipation of their saviors, the soldiers of the Holy League, whose presence rekindled the faltering embers of their resistance.

As Sobieski's forces drew nearer, the promise of deliverance began to overshadow the fear of impending doom. The skies seemed to echo the beating drums of medieval armies, while the ground reverberated with the thunderous cavalry hooves. The sight of the Holy League's arrival sent a tremor through the Ottoman ranks, instilling doubt where once only certitude reigned. Mustafa Pasha, who had nurtured dreams of triumph, was now confronted by an adversary whose zeal was bound by faith and underpinned by defiance.

It was under such portentous omens that the initial Ottoman assault reached its fierce crescendo, the clashing of swords and the boom of artillery harmonizing in a symphony of conflict that seemed to besiege the very heavens. The air was rich with the scent of battle, a bitter elixir that told tales of bravery, sacrifice, and relentless ambition. Through it all, the vigor of the Viennese defenders and the advancing knights of Christendom intertwined in an intricate ballet of salvation and sovereignty.

The stage was thus set for a confrontation that was as much spiritual as it was temporal. Amidst the din of war, whispers of legends and the invocation of divine favor were almost palpable. The defenders, standing resolutely at the gates, executed a stratagem as ancient as humanity itself: the stubborn refusal to yield; for they were not merely defending stones and mortar, but the sanctity of their faith and the future of Europe itself.

Now poised on the precipice of either annihilation or salvation, the besieged city of Vienna awaited the resolution of this epoch-defining struggle. As the stars punctuated the firmament and the wearied defenders clung to their remaining strength, the onset of dawn promised more than the renewal of another day—it heralded the decisive clash that would determine the fate of Christendom.

Sobieski's Tactical Brilliance

The mist of dawn clung to the hills around Vienna, shrouding the movements of men in armor and the tension that seeped through the ranks of both armies. As the Ottoman Empire pounded at the gates of Christendom, a savior emerged from the mists. John III Sobieski, that indomitable King of Poland, understood well the gravity of his task. Upon his brow rested not merely a crown of earthly authority, but the weighty mantle of divine purpose. His every move, every calculated decision, bespoke a sagacious mind attuned to both the art of war and the whispers of the celestial realm.

Sobieski did not stride into battle with the arrogance of one who misconstrues valor for invincibility. Rather, he approached each skirmish with the considered intellect of a master chess player. Every maneuver was a piece in a grander stratagem, meticulously designed to outflank, outwit, and overwhelm the Ottoman forces. It was not merely the physical prowess of his troops that Sobieski wielded, but a profound tactical brilliance that became legendary on the fields of Vienna.

The initial Ottoman assault was fierce, their Janissaries and mounted archers striking with a ferocity that sought to overwhelm the beleaguered defenders. Yet Sobieski had anticipated this onslaught. He had studied the art of war and understood that patience often precedes victory. For him, the battle began not with the clanging of swords, but with the silent orchestration of his forces. He fortified weaknesses, realigned troops, and ensured that his knights—those valorous Husaria—were poised for a decisive charge.

The Ottoman Turks, entrenched and seemingly infallible, suffered from overconfidence—a fault Sobieski exploited with meticulous precision. Knowing their penchant for headlong assaults, he employed feigned retreats, drawing the Ottomans into traps sprung with perfect timing. These tactical withdrawals were not acts of cowardice, but carefully laid stratagems that lured the Ottoman forces into untenable positions. Once committed, they found themselves hemmed in by Polish cavalry and crossbowmen, their retreat paths cut off and their lines of communication severed.

In the heat of battle, Sobieski's commands rang clear as a bell. The Polish King knew the power of morale and led from the front, his presence a beacon to his men. Charging ahead with the wings of the Hussars unfurled like avenging angels, he shattered the myth of Ottoman invincibility. This was no ordinary cavalry charge; it was a manifestation of divine providence, driven with unyielding resolve to reclaim what was sanctified. The sight of Sobieski at the vanguard, lance in hand, inspired an almost supernatural courage in his troops.

His tactics were not solely predicated on brute force, for Sobieski was deft in his use of synergy among various units. Infantry, artillery, and cavalry worked in concert, a triune force that leveraged each other's strengths while mitigating weaknesses. Artillery softened the Ottoman lines, breaking their formations and creating openings. Infantry advanced to consolidate these gains, holding the line whilst the cavalry prepared for their devastating charges. It was a symphony of destruction, each note orchestrated by Sobieski's genius.

Even the geography of the battlefield was an instrument in his capable hands. Hills and valleys became amplifiers of his forces' strength, choking points where the Ottoman tide could be stemmed and redirected. He utilized the environment to mask his numbers, hiding reserves in wooded areas and behind ridges, only to unleash them at the critical juncture when the Ottoman lines began to falter. The timing of these releases was impeccable, coming as hammer blows when the foe's morale was on the cusp of breaking.

Amidst the cacophony of clashing steel and the thunder of hooves, Sobieski's strategic insight shone with resplendence. He employed psychological warfare as adeptly as physical tactics. The sight of captured Ottoman standards paraded before the troops was a demoralizing vision for the enemy, while simultaneously invigorating his men with a sense of impending triumph. His communication with allied commanders was seamless, turning a coalition of disparate forces into a unified juggernaut.

In the aftermath of every engagement, Sobieski reinforced his gains with rapid innovations. Captured artillery was quickly repurposed, engineering works were erected to fortify positions, and supply lines were established to ensure the sustained effectiveness of his army. These measures were not mere afterthoughts but integral elements of his overarching strategy, revealing a mind ever preoccupied with the long game.

His tactical acumen extended beyond the battlefield into the realms of logistics and diplomacy. Sobieski ensured that his forces were well-provisioned, harnessing local resources and securing supply routes. Furthermore, he brokered alliances with other European powers, understanding that unity would be essential to repelling the Ottoman threat. Sobieski's ability to inspire and rally disparate factions under a common cause was as vital as his battlefield maneuvers.

The Battle of Vienna was not merely a military engagement but a crucible where martial prowess and divine favor melded into an inexorable force. Sobieski's tactical brilliance was the fulcrum upon which the entire confrontation pivoted. His innovative deployments, psychological warfare, and strategic foresight culminated in a victory that resonated through the annals of history.

This was not a triumph for Sobieski alone but for Christendom, a bulwark against the encroaching tide of Ottoman expansion. His actions preserved not just a city, but a civilization and a faith. Vienna remained a bastion, a citadel from which the light of Christianity could continue to shine forth. Sobieski's legacy, immortalized in this tactical brilliance, became a testament to the indomitable spirit of a king who saw his duty not merely in temporal terms, but as a divine mission.

Thus, the fields around Vienna bore witness to a theater where bravery met strategic genius. Sobieski, with every stroke of his sword and command of his voice, imprinted his indelible mark on the annals of history. Through his actions, the beleaguered defenders found hope, and through his brilliance, they found victory. The echoes of his triumph continue to reverberate, a clarion call to future generations about the power of faith, unity, and unparalleled tactical acumen.

Chapter 9: Victory in Mary's Name

Amidst the chaos and clamor of the besieged walls of Vienna, it was not the sheer might of arms alone that turned the tides of fortune, but rather the divine intercession of the Blessed Virgin, invoked fervently by John III Sobieski and his noble warriors. When the Ottomans surged forth with relentless ferocity, Sobieski, a paragon of both valor and piety, rallied his troops under the sanctified banner of Mary. In those critical moments, where the fate of Christendom hung perilously, his tactical ingenuity coupled with his unswerving devotion led to victories that were nothing short of providential. Sobieski's heart, imbued with faith, did not falter; his resolve was fortified by visions of the Virgin's grace, guiding their hands and hearts. As steel clashed and the dust of battle settled, it became clear that the triumph was not only a testament to military prowess but a profound testament to faith's sustaining power, sealing a steadfast victory in Mary's holy name.

Key Moments and Turning Points

The annals of history are replete with occasions that pivot the fate of nations. In the grand tapestry of "Victory in Mary's Name," several luminous moments and profound turning points delineate the path to triumph. As the forces of Christendom, under the venerable John III Sobieski, clashed with the encroaching Ottoman Empire, it was not solely martial prowess that determined the outcome but a concatenation of divine favor, strategic genius, and unyielding resolve.

The first pivotal moment transpired amid the shadows of uncertainty when the Polish King, ignited by an unwavering devotion to the Virgin Mary, heeded the call for aid. Here, the latent synergy between faith and duty was laid bare. Sobieski's journey from Poland to Vienna was fraught with manifold challenges, yet it underscored a vital transition—a shift from a dispersed, beleaguered defense to an orchestrated and fervent counter-attack. Each step taken by his army echoed the collective prayers and hopes of Christendom.

Upon arrival at the outskirts of Vienna, the scene was grim. The city's bastions were beleaguered, the defenders' spirits waning under the relentless siege; thus, the gravity of the moment forced a convergence of strategic imperatives. Sobieski's ascent to the Kahlenberg Heights, on the eve of battle, furnished a transformational vista both literally and metaphorically. From this vantage, the King beheld the vast Ottoman encampment sprawling below—a sea of tents and the labyrinthine entrenchments indicative of their formidable presence. This high ground instantly became a crucible where the divine interceded with the mortal.

With the initial Ottoman onslaught repelled, the defensive fortitude exhibited by the Viennese garrison played a crucial role. Nevertheless, it was the decisive Catholic counter-offensive that reshaped the narrative. Sobieski orchestrated a masterful diversion, employing the ruse de guerre with aplomb. The feigned retreat by the Polish hussars lured segments of the Ottoman cavalry into disarray, splitting their forces and creating exploitable breaches within their ranks. Herein lies a testament to tactical ingenuity, a fulcrum upon which the fate of the siege teetered.

A key juncture arrived in the form of a pre-dawn attack, chosen not by mere happenstance but through a deeply contemplative fusion of faith and military acumen. This moment harnessed the element of surprise, catching the Ottoman forces in a state of unpreparedness. The symbolism of the rising sun shadowed by Marian banners imparted a dual impetus—combating the adversary while galvanizing the beleaguered Christian forces with renewed zeal. The coalescing of militancy and piety at this moment was a microcosm of the larger battle.

The ensuing clash, ferocious and chaotic, saw the might of the Ottoman war machine momentarily waver under the relentless charge of Sobieski's legions. Here, in the heart of the melee, the fate of Vienna—and by extension, Western Christendom—hung precariously. It was during this pitched contention that another metaphysical volte-face came to pass. Reports of celestial apparitions, purportedly sighted amidst the smoke and din of the battlefield, imbued the Christian soldiers with an unearthly fervor, while casting an ominous pall over their foes.

Amidst this tumult, a singularly critical engagement unfolded—a duel of sorts betwixt the hearts of both armies. Notably, Sobieski's confrontation with the elite Janissaries, the venerated and fearsome core of the Ottoman host, is a moment steeped in legend. Their eventual rout signaled a palpable turning of the tide, as the Ottoman lines began to falter and crack, bespeaking a broader disintegration of morale.

As the battle drew toward its climax, one cannot overlook the imperative nature of coordinated efforts with allied forces. The timely synchronization with the forces of the Holy Roman Empire and the various other European contingents undergirded the multifaceted assault on Ottoman positions. This unity of purpose and amalgamation of strengths amplified the decisive impact of each maneuver. Alliances forged in faith and necessity underpinned this triumph, echoing the ancient adage—"United, we stand."

Thus, in the waning hours of conflict, another turning point loomed on the horizon. The once formidable Ottoman army, now a beleaguered and fragmented host, began its ignominious retreat. The retreat was not merely a physical withdrawal but a symbolic relinquishment, signifying an ebbing of Ottoman dominion and a reestablishment of Christian ascendancy. Following this resounding victory, Sobieski's entrance into Vienna was greeted with joyous acclamation—a moment suffused with both immediate relief and an enduring sense of divine vindication.

In retrospective contemplation, these key moments and turning points are not mere vicissitudes of war; they resonate as fundamental junctures where the interplay of faith, strategy, and fortuitous circumstance coalesced. This victory, sanctified in Mary's name, extended beyond the battlefield, engendering a renewed vigor in Christendom's spiritual and temporal domains. The fruits of this triumph reverberated through ensuing treaties and geopolitical recalibrations that girded Europe against future strife.

Unquestionably, the Siege of Vienna and the subsequent victory did not merely signify a military accomplishment but symbolized a pivotal reaffirmation of the resilience and inviolability of the Christian faith. As the embers of conflict cooled, the divine providence invoked by King Sobieski became a beacon, guiding the collective destiny of a beleaguered yet unyielding Christendom.

Aftermath of the Battle

Amidst the rubble and remnants of that fateful battleground, a peculiar stillness befell the weary warriors who had emerged triumphant. The valiant King John III Sobieski, adorned in the splendor of his blood-streaked armor, surveyed the field with a gaze that bespoke not just victory but an unmistakable providence. The clash of steel had subsided, replaced by the solemn rustling of banners fluttering under the azure sky. What transpired next would etch itself into the annals of history as a testament to both human resolve and divine intervention.

The aftermath was not merely a temporal phase of recollection and recovery but an epoch of profound realizations. The field bore the scars of a hard-fought contest—a testimony to the resolve of those who fought under the aegis of the Virgin Mary. The fallen, now silent in their devotion, were afforded rites steeped in religious significance. Priests moved amongst the soldiers, offering benedictions and solemn requiems for the brave souls who had paid the ultimate sacrifice. The atmosphere was thick with a sense of spiritual duty and reverence.

Sobieski, ever the pious monarch, led a procession to the makeshift altar erected amidst the carnage. Here, he knelt and offered thanks to the Holy Mother, whose image had graced their banners and whose protection they fervently believed had steered them to victory. His prayer was one of both humility and exaltation, a votary's testament to a faith that had fortified even the most weary of men. This act of devotion became a symbolic gesture, underscoring that the triumph was not solely of martial prowess but of spiritual fidelity.

In the days that followed, the landscape slowly transformed from a theater of war to a sanctuary of memory and rebuilding. Knighthood ceremonies were bestowed upon those who exhibited extraordinary valor, further reinforcing a culture of chivalric virtue. These new knights were not only warriors but also custodians of a moral ethos that would re-echo through Christendom. Sobieski's leadership shone brightly as he bestowed honors and saw to the needs of his weary yet jubilant men.

To the victors came not only the spoils of war but also a deeper, more existential reward—the reaffirmation of faith and divine favor. The battle had been fought with a conviction that transcended mere territorial gain or political stratagem. It was the embodiment of spiritual warfare, a crusade of righteousness against the encroaching shadows. The victory thus achieved was seen as a miraculous sign, a harbinger of an era where faith and courage would stand as bulwarks against future adversities.

Yet, within this tapestry of triumph lay the threads of poignant loss. Every victory implicates the cost of life, a fact not lost on Sobieski and his contemporaries. The narratives of fallen soldiers, immortalized in the collective memory, were tales of sacrifice that lent an aura of solemnity to the celebration. Monuments and shrines were erected to honor these martyrs, their names inscribed on tablets that would weather both time and forgetfulness. These sacred places became pilgrimage sites, where future generations would come to pay homage and draw inspiration.

Strategically, the repercussions of this battle rippled through the corridors of power far beyond the immediate theater. European capitals buzzed with the news of Sobieski's resounding victory. Celebrations erupted in courts and common squares alike, as monarchs and commoners alike breathed sighs of relief. The triumphant outcome at Vienna was not merely a defense of a city but a safeguard of European civilization from an existential threat. Alliances were bolstered, and treaties reaffirmed, as the Ottomans reeled from this decisive defeat.

The Papal states, too, offered their benedictions and heartfelt thanks. Pope Innocent XI hailed Sobieski as the savior of Christendom, underscoring the religious dimension of this military triumph. The Holy See saw in this battle a divine endorsement, a validation of their spiritual and temporal authority. Liturgies of thanksgiving were proclaimed, and Sobieski received numerous accolades, cementing his place not only as a formidable warrior-king but also as a champion of the Catholic faith.

Amid these celebrations, there was a palpable sense of providence and destiny at work. The symbolic timing of the victory, coinciding with the Feast of the Birth of the Blessed Virgin Mary, imbued the event with an almost mystical dimension. To the faithful, this was no coincidence but a celestial affirmation of their cause. It reinforced the power of Marian devotion, a theme that resonated deeply within Catholic spiritual practice.

The ripple effects of this triumph extended far beyond the immediate aftermath. Economic revitalization ensued in the ravaged areas, spurred by both the cessation of hostilities and newfound optimism. Markets reopened, and merchants once again plied their trades, emboldened by the renewed stability. The cultural resurgence was equally profound, as artists, poets, and scholars drew inspiration from the victory, immortalizing it through their crafts.

However, the battle's significance was far from parochial. It marked a turning point in the protracted struggle between the European powers and the Ottoman Empire. The Ottoman defeat served as a prelude to a series of losses that would eventually culminate in treaties that significantly curtailed their territorial ambitions. The implications were profound, setting the stage for a reconfigured balance of power within the continent.

In the broader spectrum, Sobieski's role became a pattern of virtue and fortitude, inspiring leaders and commoners alike. His leadership style, characterized by a blend of devout piety and indomitable courage, set a benchmark for future rulers. Sobieski became the quintessential Christian king, his legacy entwined with the fate of both Poland and the wider Christian world. His devotions and prayers did not merely reflect personal piety but were seen as rallying cries for a civilization under threat.

In summation, the aftermath of the Battle of Vienna was more than just a strategic victory—it was a cultural and spiritual renaissance. It reaffirmed the strength of the human spirit when aligned with divine purpose, fortifying the foundations of Christendom against its adversaries. Sobieski's indelible mark as a protector and patron of the faith became a beacon of hope and a testament to the enduring power of the Virgin Mary's intercession.

Chapter 10: Impact on the Ottoman Empire

The resounding defeat of the Ottoman forces at Vienna reverberated through the empire, shaking its very foundations and altering its course. No longer the invincible force it once seemed, the Empire faced a series of humbling defeats in the wake of their monumental loss. The treaties of Carlowitz and Passarowitz, which followed in the ensuing years, saw the Ottoman Empire cede significant territories and concede power to the European states it once threatened. The divine intervention attributed to the Marian victory and Sobieski's unwavering piety emboldened Christendom and shifted the trajectory of European history. Sobieski's triumph became a cataclysm not just for Ottoman hegemony but also for the reconfiguration of the political landscape of Europe, heralding a new era where the once-dominant crescent waned, giving way to the rising influence of Western civilization. The reverberations of this defeat were felt deeply; the Ottoman Empire, once an implacable juggernaut poised to consume the heart of Europe, found itself on a path marked by retreat, reflection, and a redrawing of its ambitions.

Series of Defeats

The Ottoman Empire, once the unchallenged behemoth striding over vast territories, eventually faced a sequence of devastating reversals that signified a turning tide in the balance of power. The genesis of these calamities can be traced back to the fateful moments that unfolded upon the battlefields of Vienna. It was there the tides of war veered inexorably against the Ottomans, marking the commencement of a series of defeats that would erode their dominion and herald a new dawn for Europe.

Upon examining the aftermath of Vienna, one discerns the myriad ways by which the Ottoman military machine began to falter. The once invincible Janissaries, stalwart defenders of the Sultan's glory, found themselves beleaguered by successive failures and the metamorphosis in European warfare. Their decline was not merely a product of battlefield misfortune but a harbinger of deeper systemic decay within the Empire.

The defeat at Vienna resonated far beyond the immediate loss of lives and territory. The psychological impact on the Ottoman ranks cannot be overstated. The invincible façade, long cultivated through centuries of unceasing conquest, shattered spectacularly. The morale of the troops and their commanders withered, as whispers of divine disfavor permeated through the ranks, casting shadows of doubt on every subsequent campaign.

Compounding these miseries were the relentless advances of the Habsburg and Polish forces, emboldened by their triumph and driven by a renewed sense of divine mission. From the gates of Vienna, the Christian coalition pursued its adversary with unrelenting vigor, pushing back the Ottoman borders and reclaiming lands that had been lost for generations. This new impetus enabled the coalition to consolidate power, changing the strategic map permanently.

One must not neglect to mention the crucial naval encounters that further decimated Ottoman power. The seas, long dominated by Ottoman galleys, now bore witness to fierce engagements with the resurgent European navies. These encounters were not mere skirmishes but pitched battles that decisively constricted Ottoman control over crucial maritime routes, further stifling their ability to project force and maintain supply lines across their vast empire.

As territory after territory fell under Christian dominion, each defeat compounded upon the last, chiseling away at the core of Ottoman strength. The once mighty Empire found itself beleaguered from within and without, forced into a defensive posture that underscored its dwindling might. The Treaties of Carlowitz and Passarowitz would later formalize these losses, yet it was the series of defeats that preceded them which had already sealed the Empire's fate.

The internal ramifications were equally profound. The Ottoman administrative apparatus, long burdened by corruption and inefficiency, found itself incapable of marshaling the necessary resources to repel the European advances. The Sultan's once-absolute power was increasingly questioned, leading to dissension within the palace and the provinces. The aristocracy, too, began to waver, their loyalties divided amidst the turmoil and uncertainty of the Empire's future.

In the broader geopolitical landscape, these defeats signified a monumental shift. Power dynamics in Europe and Asia Minor began to realign, with erstwhile neutral or vassal states now contemplating alliances that would further embolden Christendom. The Ottoman Empire's series of defeats thus became a linchpin for a wider reshuffling of power, setting the stage for new coalitions and conflicts that would shape the continent for centuries to come.

At a philosophical level, one might ponder whether these defeats were but the outward manifestations of an empire that had overreached, its insatiable hunger for conquest sowing the seeds of its own undoing. Each defeat can be seen as both a military setback and a moral reckoning, a moment when the limits of temporal power were starkly laid bare before the inexorable march of destiny.

Thus, the series of defeats endured by the Ottoman Empire after Vienna was not simply a sequence of lost battles but a transformative epoch in the annals of history. This unraveling marked the decline of a once-unified juggernaut and heralded an era of renewed Christian ascendancy. The ripples of each Ottoman defeat extended far and wide, disrupting established orders and forging new pathways for the future of Europe and indeed, the world.

Treaties of Carlowitz and Passarowitz

The tumultuous 17th and early 18th centuries bore witness to the profound shifting of power dynamics along Europe's southeast frontiers. Central to this epoch was the Ottoman Empire, whose once formidable dominance began to wane, culminating in critical junctures epitomized by the Treaties of Carlowitz (1699) and Passarowitz (1718). These treaties marked not just geographical and political reconfigurations, but cast long shadows on the Ottoman Empire's psyche and aspirations.

The Treaty of Carlowitz, etched on the annals of history in January 1699, followed a string of crushing defeats for the Ottomans, particularly at the hands of the Holy League—a coalition that included the Habsburg Monarchy, the Polish-Lithuanian Commonwealth under John III Sobieski, and the Venetian Republic. This treaty was an epoch-defining moment, not merely because it concluded the Great Turkish War, or the War of the Holy League, but because it symbolized the first significant ceding of Ottoman-controlled territories in Europe. The once unyielding walls of Ottoman supremacy now began to show cracks.

The loss of Hungary and Transylvania to the Habsburgs, Morea to the Venetians, and Podolia back to the Polish-Lithuanian Commonwealth, was more than just a territorial retreat; it was an existential blow. The Ottomans, whose expansionist zeal had been almost axiomatic for centuries, were forced to acknowledge the new limitations of their empire. The treaty, crafted under the watchful eyes of European powers, was a testament to the shifting balances, where Christendom's resolve and resurgence overcame the Ottoman encroachment.

Significantly, the Treaty of Carlowitz was also a harbinger of the complex international diplomacy of the modern age. It necessitated negotiations and dialogues in a manner unseen before, with mediators and arbitrators playing pivotal roles in achieving a somewhat tenuous peace. This not only stabilized, albeit temporarily, the region but also paved the way for the future interactions between European states and the Ottoman Empire, which were now less about wars and more about strategic diplomatic engagements.

If Carlowitz planted the seeds of decline, the Treaty of Passarowitz, signed in 1718, underscored the Ottoman Empire's diminishing influence and struggle for resurgence. The defeats suffered in the Austro-Turkish War (1716-1718) led to this treaty, mediated at a critical juncture when the Ottoman imperial ambitions faced the combined might of Austria and Venice. The treaty's terms further eroded the Ottoman stronghold in Europe, ceding territories in the Balkans and along the Danube, including Banat, parts of Serbia, and the fortified town of Belgrade to Austria.

This new territorial reshuffling further crystallized the narrative of Ottoman retrenchment. Belgrade, once a beacon of Ottoman might in southeastern Europe, now a city under Habsburg control, symbolized not just a loss of land but a plummeting morale and influence. The Ottomans had to confront the stark reality of their military and administrative limitations, especially in the face of burgeoning European unity and advances in military technology and strategy.

Intriguingly, both treaties also highlighted transformations within the Ottoman administrative apparatus. Faced with a sequence of losses and the necessity of ceding territories, the Ottoman dynasty and its support structures—viziers, pashas, and military leaders—grappled with internal dissent and the need for reform. The resultant introspection laid bare the inefficacies within their traditional systems, prompting attempts, albeit sporadic and often ineffective, at modernization and centralization.

The Treaties of Carlowitz and Passarowitz, thus, were not mere cessation of hostilities. They were harbingers signaling the slow but steady decline of Ottoman hegemony in Europe. The Empire, once the nemesis of Christendom, now grappled with the limitations of its power and influence. This period, replete with both overt and subtle shifts, became a crucible for further transformations within the Ottoman state, oscillating between attempts at revival and the inexorable tides of decline.

For Christendom, these treaties elicited a profound sense of triumph and vindication. The specter of Ottoman invincibility was shattered, allowing

European states to contemplate not just defense but expansion and colonization. The Treaties, especially Carlowitz, fostered an era where the Catholic Church, through its various monarchs and leaders, could envision and enact broader geopolitical strategies without the omnipresent threat of Ottoman aggression. The shifting power dynamics facilitated trade, cultural exchanges, and emboldened an era of exploration and intellectual renaissance within Europe.

In essence, the Treaties of Carlowitz and Passarowitz stand as monumental milestones in the historical and geopolitical landscape of not just the Ottoman Empire but all of Europe. They symbolized the transition from an era dominated by Ottoman conquests to one where European powers began to assert dominion. The resultant political cartography dictated the subsequent centuries' developments, leaving an indelible mark on the narrative of Western ascendance and the Ottoman's protracted struggle against the tides of decline.

The treaties' implications also reverberate through the religious sphere. For the Roman Catholic Church, these treaties were emblematic of divine favor, perceived as victories under the aegis of divine providence. The Catholic monarchs' victories were often framed as triumphs aided by Marian intercession, casting a spiritually-inflected light on geopolitical and military successes. John III Sobieski's contribution, particularly at the Battle of Vienna, was not merely military but imbued with a sacred mission, his devout Marian devotion embodying the crusading spirit of Christendom against the infidel.

Thus, the Treaties of Carlowitz and Passarowitz were more than armistices; they were talismans underscoring a pivot in an epoch where faith and sword often converged, reshaping destinies. The ebbing of Ottoman power and the crescendos of Christendom's resurgence were writ large across the landscapes and chronicles of the time, marking these treaties as cardinal events within the grand historical tapestry.

Chapter 11: Sobieski's Legacy

The resounding triumph of John III Sobieski at the gates of Vienna reverberated through the annals of history, leaving an indelible mark on the fabric of European civilization and Christendom. In his victory, one discerns the symbiosis of divine providence and strategic acumen; not merely a clash of arms, but a profound testimony to faith's power. Sobieski's legacy extends beyond the battlefield, encompassing his unwavering devotion to Mary, which galvanized Christian forces and invigorated a continent beleaguered by Ottoman encroachments. His deeds kindled a resurgence of Christian unity and fortified the bulwarks of Western civilization, echoing through subsequent generations as a beacon of resilient faith and resolute leadership. The epitome of chivalric virtues, Sobieski's mastery in warfare and his veneration of the divine sculpted a narrative where the sword and the cross were entwined, crafting a bulwark against tyranny that safeguarded the cultural and spiritual integrity of Europe.

Contributions to Civilization

John III Sobieski, the King of Poland and Grand Duke of Lithuania, stands as one of the key figures in the storied annals of Christendom. His legacy encompasses not just his military acumen but also profound contributions to the broader tapestry of Western civilization. As we weave through the threads of his gallant efforts and strategic brilliance, it becomes evident that Sobieski's endeavors transcended the mere battlefield, shaping the trajectory of an entire continent.

Sobieski, the devout son of the Catholic Church, led armies against the Ottoman Empire with an unyielding zeal for the Christian faith. His victory at the Battle of Vienna in 1683 did more than stymie the Ottoman advance into Europe; it catalyzed a renaissance of cultural and intellectual vigor within the Western world. The triumph served as a bulwark against the encroaching empire that threatened to eclipse the cradle of Western thought, preserving the space for a flourishing of art, science, and philosophy.

One cannot overlook how Sobieski's decisive action reinvigorated a beleaguered Europe, instilling a newfound sense of unity and purpose among its many states. The kingdoms and principalities, so often riven by internecine conflict, rallied together in a common cause under the banner of Christendom. It was a rare moment of concord, illuminating the potential of a unified Christian Europe.

Imagining a world without Sobieski's intervention invites us to ponder the persistence of the Ottoman threat and its implications on future European progress. Would the Renaissance, that efflorescence of art and intellect, have cemented its place within history absent the stability Sobieski helped secure? It's conceivable that the sustained pressure of Ottoman incursions might have stifled such cultural flowering, casting a long shadow over the potentialities of human achievement.

The sanctity of Christian heritage, upheld fervently by Sobieski, served as a cornerstone for Europe's burgeoning identity. His military success at

Vienna galvanized a collective consciousness, celebrating the intricate bond between faith and national identity. This bond manifested not only in the martial sphere but also within the very fabric of societal norms and governance, nurturing a civilization steeped in Christian ethics and philosophy.

Furthermore, Sobieski's resounding victory at Vienna reverberated through the European courts, emboldening monarchs and nobility to invest in the fortification and beautification of their cities. The resulting architectural marvels, still standing as testaments to human ingenuity, owe a debt to the security and optimism birthed by Vienna's defense. Cathedrals soared, universities thrived, and a guard against the tide of Ottoman influence was firmly established.

Consider the diplomatic ripples of Sobieski's triumph that extended far beyond Poland's borders. His collaboration with the Holy Roman Empire and various Italian states fostered an unprecedented era of alliances and treaties, strengthening diplomatic ties that underpinned European stability for years to come. Such alliances not only protected against external threats but also paved the way for more profound cultural and intellectual exchanges.

From the papal courts in Rome to the scholarly halls of Paris and beyond, the resonance of Sobieski's deed was palpable. Philosophers, priests, and poets alike found a muse in the deliverance he brought, their works reflecting an era buoyed by the promise of a safeguarded Christendom. This collective euphoria can be traced in the literary and theological works of the period, echoing reverence for a king who acted as the instrument of divine will.

Sobieski's influence was not merely confined to the grandest stages of history but also touched the lives of the common man. The palpable sense of relief from an impending Ottoman threat allowed for the flourishing of local traditions, customs, and trades, thus empowering communities to thrive with renewed vigor. Agricultural practices improved, towns expanded, and markets bustled, all under the aegis of Sobieski's protective shadow.

It is prudent to recall that Sobieski's commitment to Mary, Queen of Heaven, infused his every endeavor with spiritual determinism. His victories served as a testament to faith's inherent potency to guide and inspire. This spiritual zeal was, in turn, mirrored by many in the populace, fueling an age of heightened religious devotion and ecclesiastical patronage. Churches and chapels dedicated to the Virgin Mary sprang up in celebration of the victory achieved under her sacred banner.

Lastly, Sobieski's contributions serve as a meaningful discourse on the potency of leadership finely attuned to both temporal and spiritual realms. His life was the embodiment of governance tempered by faith—qualities that many rulers who came after him sought to emulate. His philosophies on leadership and his acute understanding of the delicate balance between might and morality form an indispensable part of his enduring legacy.

Influence on Christendom

When the clarion call of Saint Mary resonated across the plains of Vienna, it was not merely the city that stood fortified, but the very bastions of Christendom itself. John III Sobieski's leap into the fray was far more than a tactical maneuver; it was a divine imperative that reoriented the trajectory of European Christian states. His victory, shimmering like a divine jewel in the crown of Mary's favor, reshaped the spiritual and political landscape of a continent teetering on the edge of an abyss.

Sobieski's triumph bore the imprint of providential endorsement, transforming him into an emblem of divine resilience and Catholic devotion. His battlefield prowess was complemented by an unwavering faith that manifested as both sword and shield against encroaching darkness. The victory sent a resounding message: God's grace, invoked through the intercession of Mary, was an unyielding force that could rally Christendom to unite against the common threats.

The Polish king's fervent Marian devotion can hardly be understated. He entered Vienna with the decree, "Venimus, Vidimus, Deus Vicit"—a profound declaration that signified divine intercession in human affairs. The phrase reverberated through the corridors of Europe, rekindling a collective faith among its Christian denizens. Sobieski's piety, a beacon in an era steeped in turmoil, fortified the ecclesiastical authority of the Catholic Church, imbuing temporal victories with eternal significance.

This heroic defiance of the Ottoman forces, underpinned by spiritual rigor, breathed new life into European Catholicism. The successes of Vienna prompted a revitalization of the faith, energizing laypeople and clergy alike. The devout recognized that Sobieski was not merely a king but an instrument chosen by Providence to re-establish the sanctity of Christendom. Consequently, church attendance surged, and a renaissance of Christian art and culture began to unfold, influenced by this newfound fervor.

Furthermore, Sobieski's alignment with papal objectives earned him the undying reverence of Popes and bishops. His victory solidified the geopolitical significance of the Holy League, reinforcing the unity of Catholic states under the spiritual aegis of the Vatican. For the papacy, this affirmation of providential aid served as a rallying cry, rejuvenating its influence over disparate monarchies and territories that now saw the Holy See as an unassailable anchor of Christendom.

One must marvel at how Sobieski's deeds emboldened the Christian intellectual climate of the time. His military strategems were dissected and revered in academies and universities throughout Europe. Scholars began perceiving strategy and faith as interwoven, fostering an intellectual convergence where reason was seen through the lens of divine providence. This synthesis advanced theological reflection and scholarly inquiries into the socio-political roles of divine intervention.

Sobieski's influence seeped into the crevices of popular Christian consciousness, morphing legends and folklore. Songs and tales extolled his bravery, often linking his valor to divine miracles. As oral traditions morphed into written narratives, the king's saga was immortalized in ballads, chronicles, and even ecclesiastical sermons. These literary endeavors perpetuated his legacy, inextricably linking his name with the salvific power of intercessory prayer and action.

The king's victory also had profound repercussions for the concept of Christian kingship. Monarchs across Europe were inspired to view their thrones not merely as seats of political power, but as sacred trusts imbued with divine purpose. Inspired by Sobieski, they endeavored to rule with a blend of martial vigor and devout piety, acknowledging that their temporal power was sanctioned by, and accountable to, a higher authority.

The ecclesiastical impact reverberated through canon law and doctrinal teaching. The success at Vienna, attributed to Mary's intercession, invigorated Mariology within Catholic theology. This bolstered the role of the Virgin not only as a figure of veneration but also as an active agent of historical change. The Marian feasts and devotions saw an uptick, emphasizing the Virgin's unparalleled intercessory role in communal and individual sanctity.

Indeed, Sobieski's acts infused a spirit of renewed zeal within the broader framework of the Counter-Reformation. His deeds validated the triumphs of the Catholic Reformation, encouraging theological and doctrinal firmness against Protestant critiques. In this light, Sobieski's legacy was not confined to physical battlegrounds alone but extended into confessional disputes, providing a rallying point for unwavering Catholic orthodoxy.

Moreover, his victories and their attributed divine intervention emerged as an antidote to the political fragmentation that plagued Europe. Sobieski's rallying of the Holy League provided a template for multilateral Christian alliances against common foes. This notion of collective security underscored by shared faith perpetuated through subsequent centuries, evolving into political and military coalitions inspired by shared Christian values.

As Sobieski rode through the gates of Vienna, his actions underscored a philosophical resoluteness that transcended the immediate moment. This was not a mere battle; it was a cosmic confrontation between good and evil, a Manichean dichotomy fixed in the soul of Christendom. Sobieski's triumph signposted an existential vindication of the Christian ethos, a reaffirmation that, despite adversities, faith and righteousness hasten divine favor.

The ripples of Vienna's defense prompted an invigorated missionary zeal. Europe's success in repelling a significant Ottoman threat inspired clerical orders to intensify their evangelistic efforts. The Jesuits, Dominicans, and Franciscans scaled new heights in their mission work, emboldened by the vindication of their faith seen in Sobieski's triumph. This missionary expansion had cardinal implications for the spread of Christianity beyond the European continent.

In ecclesiastical architecture and art, the Victory of Vienna became a recurring motif. Churches erected in subsequent years bore icons and frescoes depicting Sobieski's valor, illustrating the interpretive fusion of martial and spiritual triumph. The architectural symbolism reinforced national and spiritual identity, serving as tangible reminders of divine intercession in the public and private lives of the faithful.

The legacy of Sobieski's victory influenced ecclesiastic, political, and cultural dialogues, embedding itself permanently in the collective memory of Christian Europe. Schools and universities integrated these historic moments into their curriculums, teaching generations the indispensable value of divine trust and human valor united against existential threats.

Crucially, the victory cast a long shadow over subsequent Catholic-Protestant relations. It served as a reconciliatory narrative, focusing on shared Christian values against a common external adversary. Sobieski's actions offered an ecumenical respite wherein doctrinal differences were momentarily set aside in favor of collective religious defense. This moment set a precedent for future dialogues, underscoring the potential of unity in diversity.

Thus, the ebullient spirit of Sobieski's victory soared beyond his era, galvanizing European Christendom in successive ages. His legacy wasn't merely

Chapter 12: The Triumph of Faith

The saga of John III Sobieski's defense against the Ottoman peril did not merely culminate in a military triumph but resonated as a profound testament to the strength of faith and fervent Marian devotion. Sobieski, rallying under the auspices of the Blessed Virgin, forged a legacy that reverberated through the annals of Christendom, transforming the siege of Vienna into an emblematic victory. This event fortified the spiritual unity of Europe, galvanizing its resolve against encroaching heresy and foreign dominion. The Virgin Mary's intercession, invoked with undying faith, manifested not merely in the overthrow of a formidable foe but ushered in an era where faith became the citadel of civilization. Sobieski's indomitable spirit and his unwavering belief in divine providence wove a narrative where the steel of swords paled in comparison to the might of unwavering faith. Such was the profound and ineffable triumph that reshaped Europe's spiritual and geopolitical landscape for generations to come.

Significance of Marian Devotion

The Triumph of Faith is gilded not by mortal arms alone but by a profound, celestial embrace. At the heart of this sacred narrative lies the fervent devotion to the Blessed Virgin Mary, a cornerstone of Catholic piety that provides both a spiritual bulwark and an emblematic anchor. Marian devotion, woven into the tapestry of the Church's history, surfaces as a beacon of light in times of strife, guiding the faithful through tempestuous seas.

The devotion to Mary finds its roots securely planted in the Annunciation, where her fiat became the conduit of divine grace. Yet, it is in the chronicles of conflict, particularly in the epoch of John III Sobieski, that we witness the wondrous fruits of this devotion in the temporal realm. Sobieski's unwavering veneration for the Mother of God was not a mere act of personal piety but a strategic and inspirational force intertwined with his military and political endeavors.

In the grand tapestry of Christian victory, especially at the Battle of Vienna, Marian devotion emerges as both the shield and sword. On September 12, 1683, as the forces under Sobieski's command faced the formidable Ottoman threat, the King's unshakeable faith in the Virgin acted as a rallying cry for the beleaguered Christian soldiers. The invocation of Mary's name stirred the hearts of warriors, infusing them with a courage that transcended the mere mortal plane.

This wasn't just about invoking divine intercession; it was a profound act of placing one's trust in the Mother of God. Sobieski's army marched under banners emblazoned with her image, their confidence fortified by prayers and hymns dedicated to her honor. In that critical moment, the battlefield was transformed into a sacred theater where earthly struggles and heavenly advocacy converged.

The victory at Vienna, hailed as a triumph of faith, resonated across Christendom. Marian devotion's providential role became a testament to the Queen of Heaven's intercessory power. This victory wasn't simply a martial success; it was perceived as a divine endorsement, a celestial nod affirming the righteousness of the Christian cause. The Mother of God's image, carried into battle, became a symbol not just of hope, but of the divine favor bestowed upon those who place their trust in her.

The perennial reverence for Mary is deeply rooted in Catholic tradition, finding expressions in liturgy, art, and personal devotion. Her titles, "Mother of Mercy," "Queen of Heaven," and "Our Lady of Victory," encapsulate the various dimensions of her intercession. These titles, far from being ornamental, reflect her profound role in the life of the Church and its faithful. Throughout the annals of history, countless saints, theologians, and mystics have extolled her virtues and urged the faithful to seek her maternal guidance.

In times of socio-political turbulence and ecclesiastical challenges, Marian apparitions and devotions have served as divine interventions, redirecting human history towards paths of reconciliation and faith. Historically, the Church has faced numerous adversities, both from within and without. Yet, in these crucibles of faith, the Mother of God has recurrently appeared as a beacon of solace and fortitude. Her appearances at places like Lourdes, Fatima, and Guadalupe have reinvigorated the faithful, presenting clear signs of divine proximity and maternal concern.

What makes Marian devotion particularly significant in the context of the Battle of Vienna and Sobieski's reign is its role in galvanizing both leaders and laity. This devotion was not a peripheral aspect of religious life but was deeply interwoven into the socio-political fabric. The rosary, processions, and Marian feasts became intrinsic to the community's spiritual armor, especially in times of impending doom. The Feast of Our Lady's Assumption, occurring just before the decisive battle, imbued the soldiers with renewed zeal, a celestial reminder of divine omnipresence.

Johan Sobieski's personal devotion to Mary was a microcosm of the broader Catholic experience. His life exemplified the harmonious blend of chivalric valor and a spiritual dedication that resonated with his people. By publicly placing his fate and that of his kingdom under Mary's mantle, Sobieski not only fortified his own resolve but also inspired a collective faith, uniting his subjects under a common spiritual cause. This collective faith, symbolized by Marian devotion, was instrumental in the unification and mobilization against the Ottoman forces.

Marian devotion serves as an invincible fortress, fostering resilience against adversities. It's an embodiment of the Church's maternal dimension, offering the faithful a touchstone of compassion and intercession. As articulated by numerous Church Fathers and Doctors, Mary's role as Mediatrix finds its essence in these moments of historical significance, where her intercession bridges the temporal and the divine.

The long-term effects of such devotion cannot be overstated. The triumph at Vienna, attributed to Mary's intercession, elevated her status immediately but also left a lasting impact on the culture and spirituality of Europe. Marian shrines and altars proliferated, each serving as a testimony to the collective memory of divine intervention. In art and hymnody, stories of Marian intercession flourished, embedding themselves in the spiritual psyche of Christendom. The rosary, already a staple of personal devotion, became a collective spiritual exercise, uniting the faithful in a shared litany of hope and gratitude.

Thus, the significance of Marian devotion in the grand episode of the Triumph of Faith transcends the temporal bounds of victory at Vienna. It encapsulates an enduring testament to the Church's unwavering belief in the maternal care of the Blessed Virgin. Her role, ever-present and ever-vigilant, continues to shine as a beacon, guiding the faithful through the vicissitudes of history. Through Marian devotion, the Church not only finds solace and strength but also a profound affirmation of divine love and protection, a testament that the Queen of Heaven watches over her children, guiding them towards eternal triumph.

Long-term Effects on Europe

The triumph at Vienna echoed across the continent, a testament not only to military might but to the enduring power of faith. John III Sobieski's victory was a turning point that reverberated through the very foundations of European society, casting long shadows over the centuries that followed. The immediate tremors of this triumph were felt palpably, but its enduring legacy lay in the transformation of Europe's spiritual, political, and cultural landscape.

The reaffirmation of Catholicism as a dominant force had profound implications. At a time when religious certainties were assailed by heresies and the encroachments of Islam, the victory reinstated a semblance of divine providence beholding to the Catholic faith. The Marian devotion that permeated Sobieski's campaign became emblematic of the spiritual resilience that held Christendom together. It reaffirmed the belief that Europe's survival was entwined with fealty to the Virgin Mary, who was seen not merely as a divine figure but as a celestial orchestrator of victory.

This period saw an invigorated Catholic Church that regained confidence in its mission. Seminaries flourished, and ecclesiastical scholarship experienced a renaissance spurred by the notion that divine favor had been visibly manifested on the battlefield. Churches dedicated to Mary sprang up across the continent, serving as physical reminders of the victory and ensuring that the devotions were perpetuated through generations.

Politically, the triumph at Vienna marked the waning of Ottoman influence and the beginning of a recalibration in the balance of power. The subsequent treaties paved the way for a stable Europe where borders were more clearly defined, reducing the looming threat of invasions which had plagued the continent for centuries. This newfound stability provided fertile ground for the growth of nation-states, each imbued with a renewed faith in their cultural and religious identities.

Economically, the cessation of constant threats ushered in an era of trade revival. Trade routes once perilous became arteries of prosperity. With commerce less encumbered by warfare, European economies could begin to flourish, giving rise to a burgeoning middle class whose impact would shape the continent's political and social reforms in centuries to come.

Intellectually and culturally, the shift was no less significant. A narrative woven around divine intervention and victory fostered a distinct and certain identity in art and literature. Paintings, literature, and music celebrated the deliverance of Christian Europe, with Marian motifs becoming ubiquitous. This provided a cultural continuity that bridged the medieval past and the dawn of the Enlightenment, engendering a shared historical consciousness.

The most profound transformation was arguably societal. The victory did more than cement Sobieski's legacy; it reinvigorated the European spirit of unity and reinforced an identity steeped in resilience. Societies became more cohesive, uniting under shared triumphs, beliefs, and collective memories. This unity, though frequently tested, stood as a bulwark against external adversaries and internal strife alike.

Religious festivals and public commemorations were thus not mere acts of remembrance but became integral to the cultural fabric of Europe. Annual rituals reinforced civic and religious identities, allowing every generation to relive the triumph, a spiritual and communal anchoring point that persisted through the vicissitudes of history.

Sobieski himself, immortalized as a paragon of Catholic valor, became an exemplar across Europe. Monarchs and leaders drew inspiration from his piety and martial prowess, and his adherence to Marian devotion spread among nobility and clergy alike. The ideal of the warrior-king devoted to faith and fatherland took root, influencing the ethos of subsequent European rulers.

Even beyond immediate religio-political realms, scientific and exploratory ventures often bore the imprimatur of this Marian invincibility. The notion of divine favor emboldened European endeavors across uncharted territories, fueling the Age of Discovery. This indomitable spirit saw the birth of new worlds, both in the physical sense and in the realms of knowledge and innovation.

The cascading effects on Europe's collective psyche led to a reevaluation of past defeats and challenges. What once were seen as existential threats became interpreted as divine trials, molding Europe into a realm destined to triumph through faith. This perspective fed into the broader philosophy that underscored the 'Christian mission' which propelled the continent's later imperial forays.

Thus, the winds of triumph that blew from Vienna did not merely scatter the Ottomans; they sown seeds of a renewed European ethos. This ethos carried with it an assertiveness rooted in faith, an unyielding conviction in a providential path laid out by divine hands. The ethos shaped diplomacy, policies, and even continental identity, invoking a comprehensive reimagining of Europe's role in a divine narrative.

No less important was the psychological bulwark built against future incursions. The fear that had once paralyzed cities and monarchs was now replaced by an optimism armed with historical precedent. The defensive mindset gave way to a more proactive stance in both territorial and theological matters, anchoring Europe's defensive and expansionist strategies for centuries.

The echo of Vienna's bells thus found a rhythm in the pulses of all European hearts. It was not a mere historical moment but a lasting cadence that underscored the drumbeat of European progress, faith, and identity. Sobieski's triumph and the Marian intercession thus imbued Europe with a redolent mixture of purpose and providence, echoing into the halls of history as a beacon of Christian resilience and unity.

In summation, the long-term effects of the victory at Vienna under Sobieski were profound, weaving into the very tapestry of European spiritual, political, and cultural existence. The sly foxes knew well that the dens of the righteous would remain ever vigilant, fortified by faith, fervor, and the undying spirit of Marian devotion.

Conclusion

The annals of history are inscribed with the valor and victories of countless men and nations, but few events shine as luminously as the triumphs in Mary's name and the legacy of John III Sobieski. As the sun sets upon our narrative, a profound reflection emerges on the entwined destinies of man and faith, which culminated in a pivotal moment for civilization and Christendom.

Sobieski's march to Vienna was not merely the advance of a disciplined army; it was a pilgrimage of piety and patriotism. The swift mobilization from the plains of Poland, spurred by an unyielding sense of duty both to his God and his people, demonstrated that Sobieski was not only a monarch but a guardian of Christendom. His devotion to the Virgin Mary shaped every decision, revealing the indelible link between faith and leadership.

This devotion was poignantly symbolized by the significance of the Feast of Our Lady's Assumption. It was more than a holy day in the liturgical calendar; it became a rallying cry that united men from diverse lands under a sacred banner. The morale of Sobieski's forces was infused with zeal, not for earthly glory, but for the holy purpose of defending Christendom against a formidable foe.

The siege of Vienna was thus a fulcrum upon which the scales of history pivoted. Sobieski's tactical acumen, though pivotal, is unerringly connected to his faith. It was in the initial Ottoman assault that his brilliance shone most brightly, catching the enemy unawares and turning the tide with decisive, almost providential, maneuvers.

In retrospect, the battle was marked by key moments and turning points that framed a narrative of divine favor. The clash at Kahlenberg remains immortalized not only in strategy books but in the hearts of the faithful, a testament to how faith can galvanize and guide leadership. The aftermath of the battle did more than reclaim a city; it heralded a series of defeats for the Ottomans and a recommitment to European unity under the Christian banner.

One must ponder the broader impact on the Ottoman Empire, which faced an irrevocable downturn following their loss. The treaties that ensued, particularly Carlowitz and Passarowitz, were more than instruments of peace—they were harbingers of the shifting dominance from East to West, a rebalancing initiated by the steadfast resolve of a Catholic King.

In examining Sobieski's legacy, one discerns contributions that transcended the battleground. His influence on civilization was profound, fostering a reinvigoration of cultural and intellectual pursuits within a fortified Christendom. Sobieski's valorous leadership and devout Marian devotion served as exemplars for generations to come, shaping not only the geopolitical landscape but the spiritual psyche of Europe.

Reflecting on the significance of Marian devotion, it's clear that such faith had a rippling effect on European consciousness. Sobieski's unwavering commitment to the Virgin Mary wasn't isolated piety but a beacon for other leaders and common folk alike. This collective spiritual reinforcement lent fortification to a continent weary of strife, providing a unifying vision that spanned beyond the immediacy of conflict.

This triumph of faith, encapsulated by Sobieski's victory and the subsequent stabilization of Europe, underscores the profound impact that a singular event can wield over the long term. The battle for Vienna, undergirded by spiritual fervor, projected a continuum of influence that shaped subsequent centuries. The reverberations of Marian devotion echoed through liturgy, art, and statecraft, attesting to the imperishable bond between belief and societal progress.

Thus, as we draw the curtain on this exploration, the intertwining legacies of John III Sobieski and the venerated Mother of God resound through the corridors of time. Their story accentuates the essence of human endeavor elevated by divine purpose. In the theater of history, amidst the clash of swords and the chorus of prayers, the ultimate victory is not merely in conquests remembered but in the enduring light cast upon civilization by faith and valor.

Appendix A: Appendix

The appendix in this tome serves not merely as a repository of documents and translations, but as a treasury of truth that undergirds the grand narrative of John Sobieski's undeniably pivotal role in shaping the destiny of Christendom. Herein are found the primary sources that lend authenticity to our account, ranging from annals penned by contemporaneous scribes to decrees issued by ecclesiastical councils. These documents, translated with meticulous care, provide incontrovertible evidence that the defense of Vienna and the subsequent victories were indeed orchestrated under the sacred invocation of Mary's name. As a lighthouse guides mariners through stormy seas, so too does this appendix illuminate the historical record, ensuring that Sobieski's valor and devotion to the Virgin Mary are venerated and understood in their full dramatic and spiritual splendor.

Primary Sources and Translations

The annals of history, particularly those concerning the Siege of Vienna and the heroics of John III Sobieski, are meticulously recorded through various primary sources and translations. These documents offer invaluable insights into the events that shaped Europe and Christendom, capturing the essence of a pivotal era with rich, unvarnished detail.

Among the primary sources are the chronicles penned by contemporaneous historians and scholars, whose discerning eyes bore witness to the epochal moments of conflict and triumph. For instance, the letters and diaries of those who fought alongside Sobieski provide first-hand narratives suffused with the raw emotions and acute observations that only battlefield accounts can offer. Merging both military and personal interests, these writings shed light on the strategies employed and sacrifices made in the name of faith and civilization.

The voluminous correspondence of Jan III Sobieski himself stands as a testament to his tactical genius and unyielding devotion. His missives to civic leaders, military officers, and the Catholic hierarchy convey not just plans and orders, but heartfelt appeals and reflections. They reveal a man driven by both duty and devotion, elucidating his motivations and his steadfast commitment to Marian worship. Such documents elevate our understanding of Sobieski from mere legend to the multi-faceted figure his contemporaries revered.

Equally critical are the official records of the Polish-Lithuanian Commonwealth and allied European states. These documents offer a broader geopolitical context, illustrating the intricate web of diplomacy, alliances, and enmities that framed the response to the Ottoman threat. Decrees, treaties, and military dispatches illuminate the machinery of statecraft and the collective will that marshaled Christendom's forces against a formidable adversary.

Translations serve as bridges, enabling modern readers to access these ancient texts across the linguistic divides of time and space. Yet, translation is an art fraught with complexity. Each translator brings their own perspective, and the choices they make can subtly alter the text's meaning and emphasis. The fidelity and interpretative nuance of translators, whether they translated from Latin, Polish, Ottoman Turkish, or other languages of the period, play a crucial role in preserving the authenticity of the original documents while rendering them comprehensible to contemporary audiences.

One cannot overlook the religious texts and sermons that pervaded this era, reflective of the spiritual ardor that underscored the conflict. The homilies that rallied troops, the prayers beseeching divine intervention, and the exegeses that framed the battle as a cosmic struggle between good and evil—all these texts are indispensable for understanding the Siege of Vienna's deeper significance. These sources are often rich with allegory and symbolism, imbuing the historical events with a transcendent quality that speaks to the enduring power of faith.

Translations of these religious texts, undertaken with scrupulous care, allow us to grasp not just the literal words but the spirit and fervor that animated these sermons and prayers. Whether it is the invocation of the Virgin Mary or the moral exhortations of the clergy, these documents weave a narrative that is as much about spiritual belief as it is about martial valor.

Besides written documents, one must also consider artistic portrayals and oral traditions preserved through generations. Visual representations—paintings, tapestries, and sculptures—provide a visual narrative that complements the textual accounts. They often encapsulate the zeitgeist of the time, presenting heroic and divine figures in a manner that text alone might struggle to convey. These artistic primary sources are essential for a holistic comprehension of the events and personas enshrined in this historical saga.

Moreover, folk songs, ballads, and oral poems captured and perpetuated by bards and troubadours offer a glimpse into the popular consciousness of the era. These oral traditions, later committed to writing, crystallize the myths and legends that coalesced around the Siege of Vienna and John III Sobieski. They embody the collective memory and communal values of the people, situating historical events within the broader tapestry of cultural identity and continuity.

In navigating through these diverse sources and their translations, scholars and historians undertake a meticulous process of cross-referencing and corroboration. The pursuit of historical truth mandates a rigorous approach to validating these accounts, discerning potential biases, and situating them within their proper historical and cultural contexts. This endeavor is not merely an academic exercise but a quest to honor the legacy of those who strove, sacrificed, and triumphed in the name of their faith.

As we delve into the primary sources and their translations, it becomes evident that they provide a narrative not just of battles and political maneuvers, but of a civilization's steadfast resolve to uphold its spiritual and cultural heritage. Each document and translation contributes to a monumental tapestry, pieced together to reflect the grandeur and gravitas of this historic epoch.

It is through these primary sources and their translations that we gain an intimate understanding of the Siege of Vienna and the indomitable spirit of John III Sobieski. These documents stand as a testament to the courage, faith, and unity that defined an era and left an indelible mark on the annals of Christendom. In studying them, we not only commemorate the past but also draw lessons and inspiration for the future.